An Introduction
to the Johannine Gospel
and Letters

Other titles in the T&T Clark Approaches to Biblical Studies series include:

An Introduction
to the Johannine Gospel
and Letters

JAN VAN DER WATT

t&t clark

Published by T&T Clark
A Continuum imprint
The Tower Building, 11 York Road, London SE1 7NX
80 Maiden Lane, Suite 704, New York, NY 10038

www.tandtclark.com

First published 2007

British Library Cataloguing-in-Publication Data
A catalogue record for this book is available from the British
Library.

ISBN-10: HB: 0-567-04584-6
PB: 0-567-03037-7
ISBN-13: HB: 978-0-567-04584-3
PB: 978-0-567-03037-5

Typeset by Free Range Book Design & Production
Printed on acid-free paper in Great Britain by
MPG Books Ltd, Bodmin, Cornwall

For

Shireen

Contents

Introduction

Reading Johannine documents is an exciting adventure that takes one on diverse roads, broad and narrow, hidden and clear, difficult and easy. Sometimes the Gospel seems straightforward to understand only to surprise the reader with its depth and finesse of expression and ideas. The reader is challenged not only by the complexities of the text, but also by the wide range of possible interpretations and approaches to it. In this book this adventurous challenge will not only take us along the road of the intriguing message of the Gospel and Letters of John, but will also venture into the difficult and often thorny terrain of the origin, the history of composition of the documents, and the external socio-religious influences that could have played a formative role in this composition process.

In the New Testament five writings are traditionally associated with John, namely the Gospel of John, the three Letters linked to his name and Revelation. In addition to these five canonical documents, John's name is traditionally linked to several apocryphal writings, for instance, the Acts of John, a Conversation between John and Jesus, various apocalypses and an unknown Gospel with Johannine elements. These apocryphal writings are primarily pervaded by a Gnostic tone and will not receive attention in this book.

Only the Gospel and the three Letters of John – and not the Johannine apocalyptic document, Revelation, which differs in style and even theology from the Gospel and Letters – are treated in this book. The Gospel and Letters have strong resemblances in theology as well as style, and have been closely related since the second century. In discussing these documents, emphasis is laid on the similarities without denying or underplaying the differences. Where there are similarities, the Gospel and Letter materials are treated together, but where there are differences these differences are pointed out. The reader will constantly be reminded about the different contexts in which the

Letters were composed and the effects these contexts and situations had on the formulation of the message.

The advantages of dealing with the Gospel and Letters together are ample. In the first place the base of information about the Johannine group and its message broadens considerably. Since the Letters were written in different situations, they apply the Johannine theology in their own way to their own particular situations. Although it unmistakably remains Johannine theology, the shifts in emphases and focus in the Letters illustrate how the Johannine theology is applied and adapted to different challenges in different situations – we have the chance to observe how the Johannine group themselves applied their message to different situations. The similarities that will be pointed out remain the golden link with the Johannine theology, while the differences will sensitize the reader to the openness and dynamics of the Johannine message.

Our adventure takes us on a journey that took the original Johannine Christians more or less sixty to seventy years to complete. This is assumed to be the time that it took for the composition of the Gospel to reach its final form. This obviously suggests a complex process of composition, not only on the level of the literary construction of the Gospel, but also on the level of the socio-cultural and religious inter-action with the contexts and situations within which this Gospel origi-nated. The Letters were also written during more or less the last two decades of the first century as a reaction to particular socio-cultural, theological and historical challenges.

There is little wonder that a variety of different methods are needed for reading these texts, covering a variety of questions related to the literary and theological structure, the origin and meaning of the concepts used, the origin of the Johannine group (circle/community/sect), the social-historical framework, and so on.

The multitude of methods used in secondary literature to analyse these documents may prove confusing if one does not make sure what the reason is for the development of each of these methods, and also how each method functions in resolving particular issues. It is worth remembering that methods are just technical instruments we use to get to answers, and motivate how we reached that conclusion relating to particular problems or issues. Different methods are developed to solve different problems. In the development of our book we will give attention to where in the process of interpretation particular methods are employed, and why they are employed at that juncture. The focus on these different methods is not for the methods' sake. As a result the methods themselves are not going to be discussed in detail, rather the book will illustrate how certain methodological approaches help to solve certain problems in the text. The emphasis is going to fall on examples of where the methods lead one, as well as on some of the results of the use of such methods.

Analysing all the different facets of the Johannine literature is a complex and interrelated process. The way that the content of the text is understood is directly influenced by the history of the composition, or one's theory on socio-cultural influences on the author(s) of the texts. If one, for instance, accepts an early date for the composition of the Gospel, a long period of development of the message is excluded, which limits the redactional and socio-cultural influences on the text. If one accepts a later date of composition, more time for influence or editorial or redactional activities is allowed for. This is an important point: making one decision has a domino effect on all the other issues. One should therefore not make hasty or uninformed decisions when it comes to the Johannine literature. Careful consideration of the different aspects related to the analysis of the text and their interrelatedness are necessary. In the end it leads one into a circular process of considering one aspect in the light of the others, constantly weighing the consequences of one's decisions. One should constantly be aware that a change of opinion on one issue may influence all the other related issues. Responsible decisions can only be taken in the light of the whole picture. It is like standing on a boat on a river. If you jump on one end of the boat the whole boat rocks. No single section is unrelated or uninfluenced by what happens in the other sections.

This obviously poses a problem for writing a book like this. Where does one start? One can only get the whole picture through laborious analysis of all the problems and their possible solutions, since only then could one weigh them in relation to one another. This implies a longer process of getting familiar with all the relevant issues, and this is what this book is all about. It wants to guide the reader through all of the different processes that are relevant to the understanding of John's literature so that the reader can develop the ability to weigh and interrelate the different aspects and come to a balanced interpretation of the Johannine literature.

One must indeed start somewhere. In this book we first focus on the text itself, trying to understand the contents and general structure of the Gospel as it is presented in the texts of the Gospel and Letters. Fortunately, the Gospel of John is a well-structured, closely knit text in which the material is thoroughly interrelated. A provisional description of the theology of the Gospel is therefore possible. While making such a theological analysis it should constantly be borne in mind that the text could and will be enriched once one starts to consider questions about the socio-cultural framework, the literary techniques being employed, the date of composition, the involvement of the Johannine group in the formation of the Gospel, etc. This book aims to lead the reader along the way to discover all the relevant information, but then both this book and the Gospel should be read and reread in the light of the acquired information – the adventure of studying the Johannine literature therefore never ceases.

What can the reader expect? The adventurous journey will depart with a discussion of the development of the message through the Gospel and Letters. A theological analysis of the text itself will follow, describing how the different theological issues are interrelated in the text itself. The literary placement of the text will then come under scrutiny – the link with other canonical documents, like the synoptics and the Old Testament will be considered to determine whether the Gospel of John is based on those traditions or whether it offers its own independent tradition of early Christianity. Concluding that it is indeed a unique document with its own characteristics, the stylistic and literary characteristics that make the Gospel such an exciting text to read will be discussed. But where do these characteristics and the unique ideas in the Gospel and Letters come from? Attention will then shift to the history of composition, which took many decades to reach completion in the final Gospel we have today. Different people and diverse influences all played a role in the composition of the Gospel over a long period. Now the important question may be asked: where did the author of John get his ideas from? Did he take them over from other religions or did he only use similar words by filling these words with different meanings? What lies behind the Johannine literature in terms of concepts and ideas? These prove to be important questions, since this socio-cultural information can enrich the understanding of the Johannine material considerably. However, if wrong assumptions on this level are made, serious misunderstanding may result.

Before we continue with our adventure of reading the Johannine literature, a few remarks about the technical presentation of this book should be made first. References to sources are limited to a minimum since the focus is not on the opinions of different people but on issues in general. The aim is to make readers aware of the important issues and some of the most important ways in which these issues are treated within Johannine research. Where central figures dominated the discussion they are mentioned and here and there a name of an important scholar is added since it is important to know that name in that particular context.

A short list for further reading is added to help the person who wants to explore the Johannine literature further. A major problem with Johannine secondary literature is that the numbers of publications are so overwhelming that it is nearly impossible just to get an overview. Fortunately, there are very good introductions, commentaries, and some standard books that could guide readers into the maize of the available literature.

When writing this book I realized how indebted I am to so many excellent Johannine scholars. So many books and people formed my views on the Johannine literature over many years. If you find any ideas similar to those of Raymond Brown, Rudolf Schnackenburg, Kingsley Barrett, Ulrich Busse, or Robert Kysar, to name a few, I most probably came across these ideas for the first time by reading their works or in discussion with them. I thank them and acknowledge them in this regard.

A brief remark about references to biblical texts needs still to be made: References to texts will be made with an appropriate abbreviation of the name of the book, except in the case of references to verses in the Gospel of John. Wherever there is reference to the Gospel no abbreviation (such as Jn) will appear in front of the numbers. In the case of references to verses in the Letters the abbreviation of the Letter's name will be used. If a series of references to the text in that Letter follows, the indication of the Letter (1/2/3 Jn) will only appear in front of the first number, i.e. 1 Jn 1.1; 2.5; 3.4.

In conclusion, I also would like to thank Dr Steve Moyise, the editor of this series, for his patience and advice, and Dr Dion Forster for his assistance with the editorial work.

1

Meeting the Gospel and Letters of John

1. Introduction

The Johannine documents are unique within New Testament literature. In their own way, they reflect on the life and teaching of Jesus, using typically Johannine concepts, expressions, vocabulary, and style. These documents were embedded into the ancient contexts within which they originated, gently touching the world that surrounded them. The footprints of the different social groups (like Jewish, other Christian, and Hellenistic) that formed part of their context of origin are evident, not only in the choice of words or concepts, but also in the way the message is formulated. Thus there is little wonder that these documents repeatedly surprise us with their unique way of presenting the message of Jesus, the Son of God (20.31).

However, before we look at the message of the Gospel, let us first get some feel for these unique documents by briefly comparing small sections of the Prologues of the Gospel and First Letter of John.

2. Briefly ... the Prologues of the Gospel and First John

Both the Gospel (1.1-18 – we are only going to look at 1.1-5) and the First Letter of John (1.1-4) start with a well-structured introduction, also called a 'prologue'. By looking at this text, the affinity between the two documents is apparent. We are not going to interpret these texts in detail but just want to observe what they 'tell' us about the challenges of interpreting Johannine literature.

The two texts read like this in translation (NRSV):

John 1.1-5

In the <u>beginning</u> was the *Word*, and the *Word* was with God, and the *Word* was God.[2] He was in the beginning with God.[3] All things came into being through him, and without him not one thing came into being. What has come into being [4] in him was *life*, and the *life* was the light of all people.[5] The light <u>shines</u> in the darkness, and the darkness did not overcome it.

1 John 1.1-4

We declare to you what was from the <u>beginning</u>, what we have heard, what we have seen with our eyes, what we have looked at and touched with our hands, concerning the *word* of **life** –[2] this **life** was <u>revealed</u>, and we have seen it and testify to it, and declare to you the eternal **life** that was with the Father and was <u>revealed</u> to us –[3] we declare to you what we have seen and heard so that you also may have fellowship with us; and truly our fellowship is with the Father and with his Son Jesus Christ.[4] We are writing these things so that our joy may be complete.

These texts have many facets:

(a) *An account of the divine entering into this world:* In the beginning was the Word (*Gr.* = *logos*) and he was God (*Gr.* = *theos*). People could hear him, see him, and touch him … and he gave those who believed eternal life (1 Jn 1). Our first steps into the Gospel and Letter are steps into an intriguing narrative of the eternal creator God and his dealings with people. We are introduced to a world where a loving God meets people in a unique way – through the Son of God, Jesus, who became human (1.14, 18). In him the divine and human came together. Methodologically we would not only need to analyse the narrative but also the theology (message of and about God) in a logical and systematic way.

(b) *The history of real people living in fellowship, but also in conflict, with God*: Through these texts we also get a peek into the history behind these texts and there we find a community who share loving fellowship with one another and with God (1 Jn 1.3-4); but there are also signs of conflict. In 1.5 it is described metaphorically: The light shines in the darkness and the darkness has not overcome it. This is a figurative way of saying that Jesus and his people witness in this world, but were not always welcomed in this world. Nevertheless they support one another through loving fellowship (1 Jn 1.3-4). An exciting trip through these documents awaits us: along the road we will meet the loving community of God, establish who they were and where the came from, but will also see the hatred and enmity they experienced. Methodologically we will have to use historical methods and approaches to enter into the history that lies behind the text.

(c) *A divine message firmly embedded in a particular socio-religious context:* Jesus is the personified Word (Gr. = *logos* – 1.1), the one who reveals the Father (1.18). This personification of Jesus is unique to John – it is not found in any other New Testament writing. However, we do find Greek philosophers, or the Hellenistic Jew Philo, using the concept of *logos* to express a mediatory figure between the spiritual and the material realities. Did the author of John form a new Christological title within Christianity by borrowing the concept from one of these non-Christian groups? Moreover, if he did, what should we make of the influence of these groups on the message of the Gospel of John? This sensitizes us to the way in which Johannine literature is indeed embedded into the ancient *socio-religious context* of its environment. We should take careful note of the traditions and influences that lie behind the formation of this Gospel.

(d) *A reality described in figurative language:* In the Word was *life* (1.4) – he was the Word of *life* (1 Jn 1.1); he was also the *light* of the world that shone in the *darkness* (1.5). Different and even contrasting metaphorical *concepts* (for instance, light vs. darkness, life vs. death) abound. Within the first few verses of the Gospel Jesus is called Word, life, and light, a sign of the rich metaphorical, symbolic and figurative fibre from which the message of John is woven. We should therefore sharpen our literary focus in order to interpret the figurative language adequately.

(e) *What remarkable style!* The literary quality and finesse of these documents should never be overlooked. The stylistic elements of these documents significantly contribute to the message, by way of emphasis, interrelating themes, and so on. Let us look at one or two examples from our texts:

(i)   The first few verses of the Gospel display a step-like structure where the last word of the previous phrase is taken up at the beginning of the next, forming a close knit structure: 'In the beginning was the WORD and the WORD was with GOD and GOD. … in him was LIFE and the LIFE was the LIGHT of all people and the LIGHT shines in the DARKNESS and the DARKNESS …' This stylistic feature semantically draws attention to the interrelatedness of these themes.

(ii) In the Prologue of 1 John there are some noticeable grammatical 'errors' with a stylistic purpose. The author speaks of the one whom they heard and touched, but uses the *neuter* instead of the *masculine* personal pronoun in doing so. He says 'IT was from the beginning, we heard IT, saw IT ...' etc., where the use of IT refers to Jesus. Initially this seems to be a crude error, but when it is observed that the author is talking about the personified Word of life, the divine one who reveals eternal life, who became a man that can be heard and touched, the stylistic reason for this 'error' becomes apparent. This stylistic technique serves to alert the reader to read carefully – this text is not only about a human, rather it is also about a divine person. It is truly a case of style 'with a message'. Structural and stylistic analysis should be an important part of the exegetical instrumentation employed by any reader of the Johannine texts.

By surveying just these few verses the multifaceted nature of these texts became evident. It is little wonder that a wide variety of methodological approaches are used in reading the Johannine texts. As readers wind their way through this book they will gradually be introduced to some of the most important methods used to analyse the Johannine texts.

3. A story with a message: the Gospel according to John

The first step in analysing any text is to get acquainted with its contents, in other words, to read it. Reading a text is a circular process, often referred to as the hermeneutic circle (spiral). You constantly acquire new information in the process of reading and rereading the text and this deepens and expands your understanding of that particular text. We are therefore first going to read the text of the Gospel and Letters as we have it. This will form a firm basis for rereading it on the basis of further theories on the development of the text through stages or on the possible socio-historical influences as well as the implications of such theories for understanding the text. Considering such theories will expand and enrich our understanding of the content of the text.

3.1 The structure of the Gospel

From the perspective of action and movement the plot of John's Gospel could not be compared to the fast moving plot of a 'James Bond' or 'Indiana Jones' movie. The movement of the plot is constantly slowed down by long discussions and monologues. In this instance it is the message that counts. As an example, except for the foot washing and the brief identification of Judas as the betrayer, chapters 13–17 are basically one long discussion. Often the only 'action' is Jesus moving from one place to another to engage in the next long discussion. Things however change when Jesus is captured and crucified in Jerusalem.

Following the Prologue, the story narrates the baptism of Jesus of Nazareth, after which Jesus calls his disciples. He then starts his public ministry, which mainly consists of him moving around, doing wondrous signs to support the authenticity of his teachings. The plot however thickens when his actions and message create tensions with the religious leadership in Jerusalem. They decide to solve their problem by getting rid of him (one can find reference to this for the first time in 5.17-18). After his eventual capture and trial he is crucified on the Friday, but rises from death on the Sunday morning. He then appears to his disciples and gives them the Spirit so that they can continue his mission in this world.

3.1.1 The stated purpose of the Gospel

The Gospel is not only a story about Jesus. It is more particularly a *message* about him, a message that tells of his significance as well as the impact he can have on people. This we read in 20.30-31, which summarizes the purpose of the Gospel:

> [30]Now Jesus did many other signs in the presence of his disciples, which are not written in this book. [31] But these are written so that you may (come to) believe that Jesus is the Messiah, the Son of God, and that through believing you may have life in his name.

The purpose as stated is twofold:

- To *believe* that Jesus is the Messiah, the Son of God. (Christology)
- That through believing, people will *have* eternal life in his name. (soteriology)

In 20.30 the reader is informed that the author carefully selected his material in order to reach his described goal. His purpose was not a comprehensive description of the history and life of Jesus, but rather to select and present his material in such a way that by reading the text the reader is brought to faith in Jesus as Messiah, the Son of God. Believing in Jesus will result in receiving eternal life. The latter remark is significant, since it marks the text as being 'performative' – it wants to do or achieve something in the life of the reader.

A hint of how this purpose is achieved comes from the immediately preceding verses where the story of the unbelieving Thomas who comes to faith is related. In spite of his unbelief, he proclaimed when he saw the risen Jesus: 'My Lord and my God!' Jesus replied, 'Have you believed because you have seen me? Blessed are those who have not seen and yet have come to believe' (20.28-29). Instead of replying to Thomas's confession, Jesus refers to those people who would in future come to faith like Thomas, without the advantage of seeing him physically in person. What do they have available to convince them of the presence of the living Lord? Thomas had the risen Jesus in front of him. What do they have? Then the words of 20.30-31 follow: 'these are written so that you may (come to) believe', like Thomas. They have the written word. The Gospel itself becomes the 'presence of Jesus' to those who read it. As the resurrected body of Christ convinced Thomas that Jesus lives, so the words of this Gospel must 'lead' the reader to the living Jesus. Yes, through this Gospel the reader is confronted with the reality of the risen Lord and his salvific message. Those who believe will receive eternal life.

People sometimes differ on the question whether this Gospel was written to bring people to faith (missionary purpose) or to sustain people's faith (pastoral purpose). This debate rests on the interpretation of the Greek in 20.31: should it read 'believe' or 'come to believe'? However, in appreciating the performative power of the Gospel, both happen. The readers are confronted with Jesus, the Son of God, but their faith is also most certainly sustained once they believe. It is a message of salvation to the world, but also a message of motivation to believers.

3.1.2 Broad structure of the Gospel

Often we read books on the Bible and not the Bible itself. The result is that we end up knowing all the theories without knowing the book the theories are about.

That is why it makes methodological sense to start with acquainting ourselves with the contents and message of the Gospel and Letters. In reading the Gospel and Letters, an important aid is to have some structure as a guide through the contents. This is especially true of the Gospel, since the frequent repetitions in the Gospel have the tendency to confuse readers who look for a logical flow in the narrative.

Obviously, every 'structure' depends on the criteria used for that particular structure. The same applies to the Gospel, resulting in different suggestions for its structure. There are, for instance, those who use references to Jesus' travels (visits to Jerusalem and returns to Galilee) as criteria for structuring the Gospel material. Others use elaborate chiastic patterns (ab–b^{1}a^1), each with different results. The most common way of structuring the Gospel is to use the particular situations in which the narrative unfolds as criterion for the order and structure. Accordingly the Gospel may be structured as follows:

1.1-18:	*Prologue*, introducing the Gospel
1.19–12.50:	Jesus' ministry to the world, i.e. his public ministry (= the world)
13–17:	Jesus' ministry to his disciples (= his people)
18–20:	Jesus' death, resurrection and appearances
21:	*Epilogue*: Jesus' final appearance; his commission to Peter.

Apart from the Prologue and Epilogue, the Gospel focuses on three big blocks of material that could each be subdivided into smaller units. Let us investigate these units now. (Obviously the following discussion can be broadened or other emphases could be chosen, but what is presented here is just a framework aimed at getting some grip on the Gospel material. What follows should be read with the biblical text.)

3.1.3 The development and flow of the contents of the Gospel
(A) Jesus' ministry to the world (John 1.19–12.50)
Following on from the Prologue, 1.19–12.50 covers the three years (according to the number of Passovers Jesus spent in Jerusalem – 2.13; 6.4; 11.55/12.1) of Jesus' public ministry. It is not what one would call a chronological account, but rather a thematic account. It is the message and not the events that dominate the narrative.

From a narratological point of view, Culpepper points out that the main thrust behind the development of the plot is described in the Prologue. Many did not accept Jesus who came to reveal God, but there were those who believed in him and became God's children (1.9-13). Tension is created with the constant resonance of sounds of acceptance being substituted and challenged by sounds of rejection ultimately culminating in the events of the cross.

(a) John 1.19–4.47: The Gospel in a nutshell
John 1.19–4.47 – usually called 'from Cana to Cana', since the first sign occurs at the wedding in Cana (2.1) and the second in Cana when Jesus heals the official's son (4.46) – may be viewed as 'the gospel in a nutshell', especially in light of the twofold purpose of the Gospel: to introduce Jesus as Messiah, Son of God, which should result in eternal life through faith (20.31).

(i) Who is Jesus?
In 1.19-51 two events, preparing him for his public ministry, are focused on, namely Jesus' baptism and the calling of his disciples. However, a closer reading reveals 'a story behind the story'. The focus does not really fall on John (the Baptist – not called that in the Gospel) or on the disciples, but on Jesus.

John (the Baptist) is solely portrayed as a witness to Jesus and he does very little apart from that. He describes Jesus as Lord (1.23); the thong of whose sandal he is not worthy to untie (1.27); Lamb of God (1.29); the one who will baptize with the Spirit (1.33); Son of God (1.34, etc.). His story becomes the story of his witness to Jesus.

With the calling of the *disciples* things are not different. Again it is a matter of a story behind the story – the calling of the disciples offers a show window for who Jesus is: It is he who is the Rabbi-teacher (1.38, 49), the Messiah-Christ (1.41), the one of whom Moses and the prophets wrote (1.45), Jesus of Nazareth, son of Joseph (1.45), the Son of God (1.49), King of Israel (1.49), and Son of man on whom the angels will ascend and descend (1.51). Through these names and titles Jesus is introduced in a colourful and varied way to the reader who now knows exactly who this Jesus is.

John 2 pictures Jesus in action at two public places, a wedding and at the temple. At the *wedding* Jesus does his first sign by changing water into wine (2.1-10); as a result 'He revealed his glory, and his disciples believed in him' (2.11). Somehow this story is more about the glory of Jesus than the taste of the wine. The bridegroom is usually responsible for the wine at a wedding. By changing the water into an abundance of excellent wine, Jesus acts as a 'bridegroom'. Jesus is the new Bridegroom of the feast of the end times (eschatology) – and if one missed this point by some chance, the author reminds one a few verses further through the words of John (the Baptist) that Jesus is indeed the Bridegroom (3.28-30).

Jesus' cleansing of the *temple* (2.13-22) and the remark that the temple should be broken down and will be raised in three days, lead to the following words of Jesus: '?But he (Jesus) was speaking of the temple of his body' (2.21). Clearly this story is not about the temple which will be broken down, but about the temple that will be raised in three days (2.19-20), the body of Jesus. And if one missed this point too, Jesus explicitly declares the redundancy of the physical temple in Jerusalem to the Samaritan woman in 4.21, 23. He is the new temple.

These introductory scenes (1.19–2.25) introduce us to Jesus, who is identified through the witness of John, introduced to his disciples through multiple significant Christological titles; yes, he is the eschatological bridegroom (who came on behalf of God) and the temple of God (who makes God present).

(ii) Eternal life is available for everybody
In John 3–4 Jesus meets with several different people, and it is the identity of these people that catches one's eye. There is *Nicodemus*, the extremely *important Jewish leader* (a Pharisee, a teacher, and a leader

of the Jews – 3.1, 10). Then there is the *problem woman*. She is a nameless *Samaritan* woman who was married five times and is not married to the man she currently lives with. She is also at the well at the wrong time of day, which implies that she did not come with the other women, for obvious reasons, not much of a letter of recommendation. In Galilee Jesus met with an *official* (most probably working for king Herod). These people have one thing in common: all three, no matter who they are, are in need of the same thing: eternal life, and Jesus offers them exactly that (3.16). Jesus shows no partiality – the life he brings is for everybody.

Whoever believes in Jesus (1.19–2.25), no matter who he or she is, will receive life (3–4). And this is part of the purpose of the Gospel – believe in Jesus and you will have life (20.31). That is why the first four chapters could be called the 'Gospel in a nutshell'.

(b) John 5-12: Jesus gives life in abundance although not everybody accepts that
After presenting the 'Gospel in a nutshell' (1–4) the story and contents are deepened. Why and how Jesus can give life is now explained in more detail (5–6). Obviously people reacted in many different ways to this novel message (7) and this gave Jesus the chance to explain to them what it really means to receive eternal life and become part of God's family – they should act according to the will of God, accept and believe in him for who he is (8–9). By following Jesus they will have a Good Shepherd who will give his life for them, but also has the power to give life to them, as is illustrated by the raising of Lazarus (10–11). Through Jesus their relation with God is restored – they are now his children and friends who can approach him freely (12). Let us take a bird-eyed view of these chapters.

In John 5–6 Jesus offers life, but how does he do it and why? The term 'eternal life' is most frequently used in chapters 5–6. Jesus heals a man at the Pool of Beth-zatha on the Sabbath and then explains why he can claim to be like his Father, giving life (5.16-24). He learned and received everything from God, his Father. His Father even equipped him not only to give life, but also with the authority to execute eschatological judgement (5.19-24). Many witness to the truth of this reality, for instance, John (the Baptist), his Father, his works, and Scripture (5.34-40). There can be no doubt that Jesus is appointed by his Father to bring life.

But how does Jesus give life? The answer is visually given in chapter 6 when Jesus multiplies the five loaves and two fish. This wondrous sign prompts a discussion about the bread of life (i.e. the bread that mediates life). By eating this 'bread', life is mediated; in other words, by sharing through faith in Jesus eternal life is mediated (6.35).

In chapters 5–6 at least two points are clearly made: Jesus has the right to give life and indeed does that, and faith in Jesus is the way in which anyone can receive this gift of eternal life and thus escape eternal judgement.

Not everyone believed this message, as we see in chapter 7. To start with, his brothers did not even believe in him (7.5), and they were not the only ones. The presence of the Son of God brought confusion among the people that became apparent in what they believed about Jesus and what they did not believe; just listen to the different reactions: He is a good man. No, he is leading people astray (7.12); You [Jesus] have a demon (7.20); Is he the Christ? (7.26); Jesus must be arrested (7.32); He is really the prophet/Christ (7.40-41); No prophet is to rise from Galilee (7.52).

Part of the confusion among the Jerusalem crowds was that Jesus offered a new way into the family of God – through faith. But what about those who worship in the synagogue and are law-abiding disciples of Moses? Are they not part of God's family? The next chapters deal in more depth with these questions of the real identity of the children of God in the light of the presence of Jesus.

A strong description of Jesus' identity introduces the discussion in chapter 8: 'I am the light of the world. Whoever follows me will never walk in darkness but will have the light of life' (8.12). The Jews however deny Jesus' testimony (8.13), showing that they do not really grasp who Jesus is. Jesus analyses their behaviour sharply: they do not recognize him because they do not know God (8.19). And now the debate is on ... who really knows God? Who can really claim to be true children of God – Jesus or his opponents?

The basic answer lies in one's behaviour, because who one is becomes apparent in what one does. A child does what his father does (8.38-39) and therefore one's deeds reveal one's family allegiance. By trying to kill Jesus (eventually on the cross) through false witness his opponents prove themselves to be murderers and liars. They are definitely not children of God, but of his opponent who was a murderer and liar from the beginning (8.44). A child of God will act like a child of God.

Jesus' influential opponents, basing their religion on the law and synagogue, denied this view and called Jesus the sinner, since he trespassed the law by healing a man on the Sabbath (chapter 9). The healed man defends Jesus by referring to what Jesus has done. Can somebody do such miracles if God is not working through him? The answer is no. Obviously the Jewish leaders did not want to accept this perfectly logical answer (illustrating their untruthfulness), so they drove the poor healed man out of the synagogue (9.34), thus proving their own spiritual blindness (9.40-41). This illustrated the point: it is not legalistic synagogue worship, but rather faith in Jesus that guarantees membership of the family of God.

Do these opponents then have a chance to become children of God on their own? No, in chapter 10 Jesus explains that he is the only door of the sheepfold of God (10.7, 9). If persons want to be part of the fold of God they should use this door. By entering this door, they will have a shepherd that is willing to give his life for them (10.11, 15), because they belong to him (10.14). They will follow the Son of God, the light of the world, the giver of life, the Good Shepherd (8.12; 10.11). Nobody will be able to snatch them out of the hands of the Father or the Son (10.29-30). Again the Jews rejected this clear message because they did not want to believe in Jesus or his works (10.38-39).

Jesus made a lot of claims about knowing God and leading people to God, but is there any proof of this pudding? Is Jesus really the only source of eternal life (8.12; 10.7, 10)? How can one be sure?

Well, if deeds are the key, then his identity must be proven through deeds. This is what the Lazarus story is about. By raising Lazarus from death (chapter 11) Jesus proves: 'I am the resurrection and the life. Those who believe in me, even though they die, will live, and everyone who lives and believes in me will never die' (11.25-26). This proves that he has the divine power to give life, as he explained in 5.21. Who can argue against that after seeing the once deceased Lazarus, now alive and walking among them? The numbers of people who started to believe in Jesus struck panic among the Jewish leaders and they finally decided to kill Jesus (11.45-53). Now the plot really thickens.

In his triumphal entry into Jerusalem, people met him as the King of Israel. What they did not realize then was that a few days later this King's throne would be a cross (12.14-15). This is an exceptional turn of events that necessitates that Jesus explain the significance of his death to his followers. He does that in metaphorical terms: like a seed that must die to bear much fruit, he must die (12.23-24). He will be lifted up on the cross and will draw all his people to him while the prince of this world will be cast out (12.31-33). Even this was not enough to convince his Jewish opponents (12.37-43).

On this note the message of Jesus to the world ends. He will now withdraw with his disciples whom he loves and prepare them for their future.

(B) JESUS' MINISTRY TO HIS OWN WHOM HE LOVED TO THE END (JOHN 13–17)
While the narrative of the first major section of the Gospel (chapters 1–12) covers three years of Jesus' public ministry to this world, the

second major section (13–17) describes events that took place during a single evening when Jesus gathered with his disciples for supper. This was the few hours before he was taken captive resulting in the events of the cross. Jesus knew exactly what awaited him.

What was the message of Jesus to his disciples before the cycle of events started that would physically separate him from them? 'By this everyone will know that you are my disciples, if you have love for one another', Jesus said (13.34-35). To illustrate what that meant in practice, he washed the feet of his disciples as a supreme token of his love for them (13.1-11). This should also serve as an example for them (13.15).

Following the meal – after Judas, his betrayer, had left into the darkness of the night – Jesus prepares his disciples for his departure to his Father. Their discussions that night are known as the Farewell Discourse(s) and can be subdivided into three parts: the first discourse (13–14) ending with the words, 'Rise, let us go from here' (14.31); the second discourse (15–16); which is followed by Jesus' prayer (17).

In John 13–14 Jesus' assures his followers that they are indeed on their way to the Father because Jesus is 'the way, the truth, and the life' (14.6) – as long as they stay in a close relationship with him they are on their way to the Father. They will not be left orphaned even if Jesus returns to his Father (14.18). Jesus will be with them in different ways. He will be with them through the Spirit of truth, their special Helper who will be sent to them (14.16-19, 26); Jesus' words and works will also be a constant reminder of his presence with them (14.10-12, 23-24). And, he will only be a prayer away from them – he will give them whatever they ask in his name (14.13-14). Indeed, his presence will be dearly felt – he and his Father will come and will 'make home with everyone who loves him and keeps his commandments' (14.23; 14.15, 21).

In chapters 15–16 it is explained why they must keep their relationship with Jesus intimate, like that between a vine and its branches (15.1-17). Only then will they bear the fruit that pleases God (15.8). Not everybody will appreciate their fruit, and some will even hate them like they hated Jesus (15.18ff.). They might even be persecuted to the point of death (16.2). But they can be assured, they will not be alone. The Spirit, their special Helper (*Gr. = Paraclete*), will guide and lead them (16.5-15). Their sorrow will change into joy (16.16ff.) since Jesus and the Father will indeed be with them. (There are a number of overlaps between chapters 14 and 16.)

Jesus addresses his Father in chapter 17. Although this prayer is often called 'the high priestly prayer' there is nothing in the context to warrant that. It is also often called the 'testament' or 'last will' of

Jesus. This comes a bit closer to what it really is. It has the character of a 'report back' to the Father of the Son who was sent on a mission by the Father. Look at the progression of the content in the prayer.

- 17.1-5: Jesus remarks that he *accomplished* the work that the Father sent him to do – to give eternal life to all those who belong to the Father. He is ready to return and be glorified.
- 17.6-8: The *result* of his mission was that many received the message of Jesus and indeed believed, forming a community of believers.
- 17.9-19: *What* should now *happen* to *these believers*? Well, Jesus does not ask that they should be taken out of this world, but that the Father should protect them in this world so that they can continue Jesus' mission.
- 17.20-23: *What* should *happen* to *those who will in future* come to faith through the word and message of the disciples? Jesus also prays for them; He prays for loving unity, not only among themselves but also unity with the Father and Son.
- 17.24-25: Jesus' explicit wish is that *eventually* all believers should be where he is – with the Father in glory.

The thematic progress is evident: Jesus completed his mission (verses 1-5) with good results (6-8). He then lays out the 'plan of action' with the Father for the believers, both current (9-19) and future (20-23). Eventually all of them will be where Jesus is (24-25).

This concludes the events at the table that night. So after Jesus spoke these words, they left for the garden across the Kidron valley (18.1).

(C) JESUS IS GLORIFIED: THE CROSS, RESURRECTION, AND HIS APPEARANCES TO HIS FOLLOWERS (JOHN 18–20)

The narrative about the cross-events (chapters 18–20) largely follows the chronological sequence of the other Gospels (Mark and Luke). Jesus is captured and questioned by both the high priest and the local political ruler, Pontius Pilate, and is then sentenced to death by crucifixion. He was then buried, but rose on the third day, after which he appeared to his disciples.

Although the chronological sequence of events is the same in the different Gospels, the presentation in John's Gospel is unique for several reasons.

(a) This is not a story focusing on suffering. Jesus is not portrayed as the powerless, suffering one, but as the one who has true power, that is, the one who has everything under control. As he says to Pontius

Pilate (18.35-38): 'You would have no power over me unless it had been given you from above' (19.11). His life is indeed not taken from him, but he willingly lays it down (as he said he would in 10.17-18). He is King, but his kingdom is not from here (18.36).

(b) His innocence and kingship are clearly declared. If one listens carefully to Pilate, he keeps on repeating two things: He does not find Jesus guilty of any crime and he constantly talks about Jesus' kingship (18.33-39; 19.3-6, 14-15). To the dismay of Jesus' Jewish opponents he even writes it down as a title on the cross: 'Jesus of Nazareth, the King of the Jews' (19.19).

(c) These narrated events are integrated with the theology of John – these events are indeed history with a message. This is evident from the brief overview of some of the themes Jesus talks about during these events: Jesus drinks the cup the Father has prepared for him – he does what the Father asks (18.11); he has no hidden agenda and speaks openly for everybody to hear (18.20-24); he is a King, but his kingship is not of this world and that is the truth (18.34-38); the power does not lie with Pilate but comes from above (19.11). Jesus cares for his mother and introduces her into the community of believers (19.26-27).

(d) Stylistically *irony* plays a very important role in these events. The opponents of Jesus are ignorant of the power game that is really taking place. They think they are in charge, but in reality the power lies with the one they think is powerless, namely, Jesus. Ironically they are crucifying the Son of God under false pretences and should therefore be the ones to be crucified, since they are the true blasphemers and murderers. Even more ironically, in the case of Jesus, the cross becomes the throne of Jesus. The title at the top of the cross declared that: this is the King of the Jews (19.19). The cross should not be seen as an instrument of suffering and humiliation, but rather the glorification of the Son of God (12.18; 17.1-5).

Although the narrative follows the well-known chronological pattern, it is presented in a unique and challenging way, combining Johannine theology with the cross-events.

(D) THE PROLOGUE AND EPILOGUE ARE BOTH SIGNIFICANT IN THE LARGER CONTEXT OF THE GOSPEL (JOHN 1.1-18 AND JOHN 21 RESPECTIVELY).
The *Prologue* introduces the reader to what follows in the rest of the Gospel. It is well structured and is usually divided into two sections (1.1-14 and 1.15-18). Verses 1-14 present the reader with a brief

historical overview, starting from the beginning, where the pre-existent Word was already there, telling about creation, the presence of light and darkness (sin) in creation, the activities of John (the Baptist) and eventually of Jesus (the Light) who was not accepted by his own people (1.9-11). Nevertheless, to all who believed in him he gave the power to become children of God (1.12-13).

In 1.14-18 the same themes re-occur, but in reverse order – Jesus became flesh, John (the Baptist) witnessed about Jesus, and Moses gave the law that had to deal with sin. However, in 1.14-18 the spiritual significance of Jesus is emphasized through words like glory, grace and truth, things that neither Moses nor John could offer. Jesus is indeed the one close to the Father and is therefore able to make him known (1.18). At this point the stage is set and the curtains are drawn for the narrative that is to follow in the rest of the Gospel.

The *Epilogue* is seen by many as a later addition. It is argued that 20.30-31 looks like the proper ending of the Gospel (since it expresses similar ideas to 21.25), that this chapter deals with the deaths of two key figures (Peter and the Beloved Disciple), and that the vocabulary differs significantly from that of the rest of the Gospel. Be that as it may. As it stands it makes an interesting contribution to the Gospel. When Jesus meets with his disciples at the Sea of Tiberias he illustrates to them that they can rely on his power and presence in their further endeavours. He then restores Peter, who had denied him, and commissions him to look after his flock, but only after Peter declares his loving loyalty to Jesus. The flock of Jesus will continue to be cared for through the love and power of Jesus. The future is open and bright.

Indeed, whoever reads this Gospel cannot remain untouched; it constantly challenges the reader … it is a real performative text!

4. What are the Letters of John about? An overview of their content

The contents of the Letters reflect a community that is in conflict about the essence of their identity and their message. (It is debatable whether 1 John is indeed a Letter. It does not have the typical introduction or conclusion of ancient letters. For convenience it will however also be called a 'letter' in this text.)

3 John differs from 1 and 2 John in content. This letter gives us some insight into the inner conflicts and power struggles within the Johannine. A conflict arose when one of the members of the Johannine group, a certain Diotrephes, refused to receive Christian visitors (who were most probably missionaries on their way) and thus challenged the authority of the elder (3 Jn 9-10). Apparently the situation was not that bad yet, since it seems as if relations were still intact. The elder indicates that he will sort out the problem with Diotrephes when he comes again. Christians who live according to the truth, like Gaius to whom the letter is addressed, should support one another, especially as the fellow workers in the truth.

The issues addressed in *1 John* are clearer than the structure, which seems to elude precise description. There is a literal link in purpose between this Letter and the Gospel: 'I write these things to you who believe in the name of the Son of God, so that you may know that you have eternal life' (1 Jn 5.13). The issues of believing in Christ and living like people who have eternal life are at stake.

A schism had occurred within the Johannine group resulting in members of the congregation leaving. The issue at stake seemed to have been the person and identity of Jesus. Expressions like, 'Who is the liar but the one who denies that Jesus is the *Christ*?' (1 Jn 2.22) or, 'By this you know the Spirit of God: every spirit that confesses that Jesus *Christ* has come in the *flesh* is from God' (1 Jn 4.2), show that the dissident group apparently acknowledged the divinity of Christ, but not his humanity. They argued that he only had the semblance of a human being (docetism). They even claimed enlightenment by the Spirit for their views (1 Jn 4.1-2), but this does not impress the author. One should not believe everyone who claims to speak through the Spirit. There are many false prophets (1 Jn 4.1-2). The author therefore refutes their views in the strongest possible terms by calling them 'antichrists' (people who have turned against Christ).

This docetic view of Christ also had an impact on the way people lived. It influenced their behaviour. For them only the spiritual dimensions actually counted, while physical things, including the body, were not important at all. It therefore did not really matter what one did with one's material body. That is why these people could walk past a brother or sister in physical need without even thinking of helping that person. There was no need for expressing love in physical terms, since only spiritual things count (1 Jn 3.11-18). The author rejects this view as false: such people claim to have fellowship with God, who is light, but walk in darkness (1 Jn 1.5-6).

However, the Letter also carries a strong positive message, similar to that of the Gospel. All who believe in Jesus are born as children of God to become part of God's loving family (1 Jn 2.29–3.10). They should live in love with one another because God is love (1 Jn 4). Through faith, they are the victors in this world (1 Jn 5.4-5).

There are many similarities in both language and content between *1* and *2 John*. 2 John is much shorter, but also expresses concerns about the wrong understanding of Jesus: 'Many deceivers have gone out into the world, those who do not confess that Jesus *Christ* has come in the *flesh*; any such person is the deceiver and the antichrist!' (7-8). Believers should take extreme care to stay on the right path. They should love one another as Jesus commanded them (5-6). However, when it comes to false prophets they should not even mix with them or allow them into their homes (10).

5. An intriguing question: what is the relation between the Gospel and Letters of John?

There are striking similarities between the Johannine Gospel and the Letters. As early as Irenaeus (180 CE) the link between the Gospel and Letters of John was made and common authorship was suggested. It is not difficult to see why. The similarities on both literary and thematic levels are striking. A few examples relating to the First Letter illustrate this (a comprehensive list is available in Brown's commentary (1983) on the Epistles):

Theme	Gospel	Letters
Purpose of writing	20.30-31	5.13
God gave his Son	3.16; 5.20	4.9; 5.11
Life	1.4; 3.16	1.2; 5.12
Light	3.19-21; 8.12	1.5-7
Love	13.34; 15.17	3.11, 23
Truth	8.32	2.21
Commandments	13.34	2.7
Follow Jesus' example	13.15	2.6
Sin	1.29; 8.46	3.5-6
Hate	15.18	3.13

Although the Gospel and the Letters were obviously written in different contexts, the conceptual and literary similarities are so remarkable that similar authorship, or at least a common source of origin (implying a different author but from the same circle), is usually accepted.

Thus, one can safely conclude that the documents are obviously related, but how should one understand the relationship? This is not an insignificant question and there are two possibilities that should be considered seriously.

(a) One approach suggests that the Letters were written after the Gospel as reaction to misunderstandings within the Johannine community based on the misreading of the Gospel by a section of the community. The conflict between the two sections within the community was so serious that it led to a schism in the Johannine group. 1 and 2 John was then written by an authoritative Christian figure in order to solve the problem by correcting false understandings of the Gospel. The implication is that the Letters are examples of how the Gospel was interpreted in later situations, which makes the Letters the 'first commentaries' on the Gospel.

(b) Another approach argues that the Letters were written somewhere before the final redaction of the Gospel. This argument is largely based on the theory of the traces of the development of the conflict within the Johannine group. In 3 John we find the Presbyter still in a position to address Diotrephes in an authoritative way. There is no direct split yet. In 2 John 10-11 we find 'opponents' who were part of the community being shown the door. It seems as if the 'opponents' had not left the community yet, but that the split was immanent. In 1 John 2.18-19 these 'opponents' who were formerly part of the community finally left and are called antichrists. In the Gospel of John we find not only the much wider conflict of the community with its Jewish opponents, but in Chapter 6.60, 66 and other places (8.31ff.; 15.2) disciples of Jesus left him and went home, which signals a final break. Based on the development of the conflict, it seems plausible that the Letters were written before the Gospel. This would imply that the Gospel should be read in the light of the Letters. The Letters show what type of problems the community was faced with while they were discussing and reformulating the tradition which found its final expression in the Gospel in its present form. This gives a different view of the history and development of the Johannine corpus.

Although the latter approach (and there are more variants) has its champions, the former approach enjoys larger acceptance. Be that as it may; reading the Gospel and Letters of John in tandem enriches the understanding of the message and ideas found in these Johannine documents. Especially valuable is the fact that the Letters were written in apparently different situations to that of the Gospel, which gives us insight into the way in which the Johannine message is applied in specific practical situations. In that sense the Letters are extensions of the Gospel of John since they give us a broader look into the Johannine group's everyday experiences. Thus our view of the Johannine group is significantly enriched.

Because of the similarities and shared tradition, the message of the Gospel and Letters will be treated together in so far as they overlap. The mistake should not be made of thinking that there are no differences. No, there are pertinent differences, from the vocabulary used to differences in theological views. These will be indicated where necessary.

A few illustrations of the latter should suffice.

(a) The Gospel is known for its *realized eschatology* – whoever believes *has* eternal life (3.15-18). Signs of a futuristic eschatology (that one will only receive life in future) are rare, for instance, in 14.3 (where Jesus will come again and take believers to the house of the Father) or 6.39-40 (where there is mention of the 'last day').

However, in 1 John 3.2 we find a much more developed futuristic eschatology: 'We are God's children now; what we will be has not yet been revealed. What we do know is this: when he is revealed, we will be like him, for we will see him as he is.' This is a clear expression of futuristic eschatology and is much more clearly articulated than in the Gospel.

(b) We do not find references to the salvific blood of Jesus in the Gospel. Neither do we find reference to the Son who was sent as expiation (propitiation/atoning sacrifice) for our sin. However, in 1 John 1.7 we read that the *blood of Christ* cleanses us from all sin and in 1 John 4.10 that God 'loved us and sent his Son to be the *atoning sacrifice* for our sins'. Again, the Letter goes further in the development of a theological theme, namely, the atonement.

(c) The use of the central theme of love differs, not so much in content but certainly in emphasis. It is never directly mentioned in the Gospel that believers should love God, but it is an explicit theme in the Letters (1 Jn 4.20-21). That God is love is made explicit in the Letters but not in the Gospel. The same applies to confession of sin made explicit in 1 Jn 1.8-10 while it is not expressed in that way in the Gospel.

Why are there differences and even expansions (like the atonement, eschatology) in the Letters? These differences could be explained in different ways, for instance, that different problems were addressed in different social situations, or that the documents were written by different authors although they were from the same 'school'.

Another factor should be remembered. It was shown earlier that the Gospel was written with a very specific Christological and soteriological purpose in mind (20.31). In order to attain this purpose a selection was made from the available material on Jesus (20.30; 21.25). It can therefore be accepted that the Gospel does not want to give a full and detailed description of all the available theological material or theological positions. It has a more pointed and clearly selected purpose. Certain issues that were not so relevant for that particular purpose were not treated or discussed. The Gospel therefore does not present us with a closed system of ideas or a comprehensive all-inclusive theology. Rather, it presents us with selected theological ideas aimed at presenting Jesus as Son of God so that people can believe and receive eternal life.

It is also true that the Johannine group was confronted with different situations and inner communal problems as we see in the Letters. In addressing these problems the author has no problem in using more orthodox ideas or views on, for instance, soteriology (the blood of Jesus or the idea of expiation) or eschatology (the futuristic element). These (expanded) ideas in the Letters should not be seen as being in conflict with the ideas in the Gospel, as if the Gospel presents us with a closed system of ideas. Rather, the ideas should be seen as broadening and enriching the theological scope in relation to the needs of the situations that arose. It could therefore be said that if the Johannine group was asked the question about the blood of Jesus or the futuristic nature of their faith they would have answered positively (as in 1 John) without experiencing a major conflict of ideas.

Thus far we have acquainted ourselves with the logical flow and content of the Gospel and Letters. Now we can move on to the next question. What does the Johannine literature teach us about particular theological themes like God, Christ, salvation, ethics or the Spirit? This process is known as a theological analysis and will receive our detailed attention in the next chapter.

2

Theological Analysis of the Johannine Literature

1. Theological analysis of the Johannine message – about method

1.1 Approaching the Gospel theologically

In the previous chapter, we followed the linear development of the Gospel from chapter 1 to chapter 21 and came across themes like eternal life, proper behaviour, sin, and faith. We also met characters like the Father, the Son, the disciples, and the Jewish opponents. However, these central themes and characters are developed in a comprehensive way throughout the Gospel. The Gospel has a way of constantly returning to the same topic in a spiral fashion. (A simple concordance search of, for instance, 'life', 'being sent', or 'love' will confirm this.) If we, therefore, really want to get a full picture of what the Gospel says about themes like Jesus (Christology) or salvation, we will have to engage in a process where we gather all the material presented in the whole Gospel (and Letters) about a single topic in a logical and systematic manner. Systematizing all the relevant material about specific topics in a responsible process of interpretation will give us an overview of the message of the Gospel and Letters. This process is called theological analysis.

However, this process of 'systematizing' the material is not as self-evident as it may seem. There is no single generally accepted way of theologizing and there are indeed different ways of doing it. We should therefore briefly describe and motivate the way the theological analysis is going to be done here.

Excursus: *Examples of some theological approaches to the Johannine literature:*
Theology of the New Testament implies a systematic, coherent, logical, and

well-motivated presentation of the essential contents of the message of the New Testament, illustrating the inner dynamics of related materials. There follow some examples of theological approaches to the Johannine theology:

(a) The information may be approached from a pre-perceived *thematical* framework (Guthrie). Specific 'themes' are chosen, like God, Jesus, sin, faith, salvation, Spirit, eschatology etc. and then these themes serve as a basis for gathering and systematizing material. The problem is of course that the themes are usually not chosen on the basis of the text itself, but rather reflect a particular dogmatic position. Material in the particular book not covered by one of these themes is not treated. Forcing the relevant material into categories is also an ever-present danger.

(b) Others approach the material from a specific historical perspective, for instance, post-Easter (Goppelt). The way in which the material is presented is then determined by this view of the *history of salvation*. The past and future only become understandable through the central post-Easter perspective following Jesus' cross, resurrection and ascension.

(c) Theologians like Kümmel are positive about the historical value of the New Testament texts and follow a consistent *historical* method. This theology consists of a positive historical description of the Jesus events. It almost boils down to 're-telling' the stories as they are found in the New Testament.

(d) Bultmann's theology was, for instance, influenced by a strong *hermeneutical* perspective. After doing a historical-critical analysis of the text, he interpreted the kerygma in the light of the existential appeal it has on the modern reader (hermeneutics of existentialism). To be able to do that he had to demythologize the text (get rid of all the signs of an ancient worldview).

(e) Hahn in his theology has a double approach. He treats the *historical* and the *thematic* aspects of the message in separate sections (volumes). He regards both as important parts of a New Testament theology and together they form the theology of the New Testament.

Theological analysis involves both the processes of *description* and *interpretation*. The available and relevant material in a particular book on a particular topic should be gathered and described based on the question: what does the text offer in relation to a particular issue or theme? This information should be interpreted within a proper methodological framework that corresponds to the nature of the relevant New Testament book (theological material is offered differently in Letters than in Gospels or histories): questions like 'how', 'why', 'wherefore', 'in what context', etc. should be asked. The logical relations between the different elements in the text should be explained and motivated. It is an effort to understand not only what the original author wanted to say, but also why, how, and on the basis of which presuppositions is the author arguing a particular point of view.

1.2 Theology and John's Gospel: relational theology

The Gospel of John and his Letters are not theologies in the way we understand it – they do not provide us with a systematized picture of God, salvation, ethics, etc. However, they present us with theological material that we as theologians should gather, systematize, and interpret. The question now is: how should we go about doing this? To answer this question we should take cognizance of the way in which this 'theological material' is available in the Gospel.

The author does not follow a strictly linear, point for point, pattern for developing his ideas. He does not first discuss one point, then another and another until he comes to a conclusion. He rather gives some information about a topic, moves on to another, returns to the first one, and so on. A major stylistic characteristic of the Gospel is therefore this repetitive way in which the author unfolds the 'theological material'. Take some major themes as clear examples of this approach:

- Life is mentioned in 1.4; 3.15, 16, 36; many times in chapters 4, 5 and 6; 7.38; 8.12; 10.10, 28; 11.25-26; 12.25, 50; 14.6, 19; 17.2, 3; 20.31.
- Mission is mentioned in 3.34; 4.34; many times in chapters 5, 6, 7, 8; 10.36; 11.42; 12.44, 45, 49; 13.20; etc.

This repetition of themes is usually labelled as the Johannine *spiral* of thought. The author constantly returns to central themes while unfolding others. It is not just a matter of repetition for the sake of repetition. The different theological topics are *developed* in *relation* to each other. The author constantly returns to the same topic but each time relating it to a different issue or topic, thus gradually unfolding and developing the whole theological picture. A Swiss scholar, Jean Zumstein, explained the repetition on the basis of a process of *Relecture* through which the traditions (material) in the Gospel were read and reread and the consequent results of these 'rereadings' were then deliberately presented (repeated) again further in the Gospel – that is why there are repetitions.

You cannot therefore with confidence claim to know what faith is, or who God is, before you have analysed the whole Gospel, since a comprehensive theological picture of God can only be drawn if all other relevant issues are considered, like what he does, how he does it and to whom, and why he performs these actions. This information is spread throughout the whole Gospel and is unfolded in a spiral-like manner. To describe a particular 'thread' (say 'God') in the theological tapestry of John, this particular thread should be traced in the whole of the tapestry, not only as an individual thread, but also in relation to the other threads (Christology, mission, faith, salvation, etc.). Eventually all the theological themes should be interrelated to form the larger theological picture. These unfolding perspectives should be analysed and explained in order to present a dynamic picture of the comprehensive theological or conceptual framework of this Gospel.

Excursus: *The pictorial nature of Johannine theology:* This way of *relational thinking* may be compared to the way in which one goes about describing a painting. Imagine you see a painting of a man sitting under a tree next to a river while the sun is setting, looking at the beautiful flowers around him. If someone asks you to describe the *man*, you would most probably also say that he is sitting under the tree, and that he is looking at flowers, etc. You make mention of the 'flowers' and the 'tree', although you are describing the *man*. The same will happen if the person asks you to say something about the *tree*. You will say that it stands next to a river, and that there is a man sitting under it, etc. The reason for this is that the different objects stand in *relation* to each other and should be related in order to give a full description of the picture. There is no logical point at which to start. You can actually start anywhere since in the end every object will be dealt with in some way. Some things are usually more in focus in the picture than others. However, in the end you will cover the whole picture in your description, no matter where you start. This is also how the theological material in this Gospel functions – one can perhaps talk of the 'pictorial nature' of the theology of John.

A final point about methodology: the theological analysis that follows, takes the above points seriously. Obviously, extra-textual material like the socio-religious context of origin, the social dynamics of the described events, the origin of the concepts used, play an important role in any theological analysis. The danger of starting with such theories is that the reader, for instance, first decides what the socio-religious background is (for instance, Gnostic, Hellenistic, or Jewish) and then continues with the analysis of the textual material in the light of this choice. This predisposes and predetermines the analysis from the start.

In our analysis we take a different point of departure. We will first follow a *descriptive* road – describing the content of the theological material in the Gospel in its interrelatedness. This is possible, since the Johannine theological concepts are well related within the confines of the text. Information gathered through this preliminary analysis should then be enriched, interpreted, and understood in the light of plausible extra-textual information. This follows in the latter chapters of this book, where it will be illustrated how the initial understanding of the theological material is enriched and thoroughly *interpreted* in the light of additional and extra-textual information.

Just a reminder: the theology of the Gospel and the Letters overlaps on many levels, but also differs. The point of departure of this description is the Gospel. From here areas where the Gospel overlaps with the Letters will be indicated. The notable differences between the Gospel and Letters will also be mentioned.

2. John's view of reality: contrasting worlds

'John's story of Jesus' unfolds within a world of contrasts: there are light and darkness, life and death, lies and truth. These contrasts form the theological presupposition for John's message. It forms the setting for John's theology, gives the reason for the coming of the Son, and motivates why there is hate instead of love, lies instead of truth in this world. Let us investigate further.

2.1 Contrasting realities

John's narrative is based on a particular view of reality that is dualistic. The universe is divided into this earthly reality, or the 'below', and the heavenly or divine reality, the 'above'. With the coming of the Word, Jesus, who is God (1.1), the 'above' entered into the 'below' so that these two realities intersected in the person and work of Jesus. Obviously, through the 'meeting of these two realities' pertinent *contrasts* between them became apparent (also known as the Johannine *dualism*, although it is not an exact dualism. The divine qualities stand in contrast to the earthly qualities, but are not of equal quality or importance. The divine qualities are far superior to the earthly qualities.)

The essence of this dualism is based on the God that existed before creation. He created everything that exists through the Word (1.1-3). This resulted in a definite and qualitative contrast between Creator and created. It goes without saying that creation should be judged in the light of the Creator. The true and authentic in creation should be measured against him; for instance, what is trustworthy and true (3.33; 4.24; 8.40); what is good (3 Jn 11); what true love is (1 Jn 3.16; 4.8, 16), etc. The value system of reality is defined in terms of, and based upon, God and who he is. This forms a basic point of orientation in Johannine theology.

A distinction could be made between *creational* contrasts (for instance, between heaven and earth, spiritual and physical, eternal and earthly time) and *ethical* contrasts (contrasts between good and evil, truth and lies) in the Gospel. These two types of contrast are not mutually exclusive, but overlap. Creation is something good that can become evil, or evil may also present itself in a spiritual way (the devil and the evil spirits – 1 Jn 4.1-2). Let us get a clearer impression of this contrasting view of reality.

2.2 Creational contrasts

2.2.1 Contrast in space – heaven and earth

Two realities can be distinguished that are 'inhabited' by different (A)actors in the Johannine narratives.

- The space referred to with the words 'above', or *heaven*, refers to where God, who is Spirit, is, to his abode with his angels (1.51; 12.29). This is also where Jesus comes from and where he is going (3.13, 31; 8.23; 14.1-2, 28).
- The abode of the ruler of this world, the devil, and also of humans, is on *earth*, also called the 'below' (8.23; 12.31). That is where the flesh is. Note that John's worldview does not include an under-world where evil lives (a three-storey universe). The devil lives in this world and is indeed called the ruler of this world (a two-storey universe).

There is a qualitative difference between the *spiritual* (Gr. = *pneuma*) and the *physical* (*flesh* – Gr. = *sarx*; 3.6) sides of reality. Nobody has ever seen God, since he is spirit (1.18; 4.24; 5.37; 1 Jn 4.12 – in spite of what the Pharisees say in 9.29) and as spirit he must be approached in spirit (4.24; 6.63). The spiritual is not directly accessible to 'flesh' and there are limitations to what flesh can do in relation to the spiritual reality. Flesh can only do, see, speak, and judge according to the nature of flesh (3.6, 31; 8.15; 1 Jn 2.16). This is not a moral 'good–evil' contrast but a contrast of quality or ability. The earthly things are not evil or bad as such, but simply *qualitatively* different. This is not a Gnostic worldview as some have suggested, because then creation must have been evil and bad.

This *qualitative* difference between heaven and earth, spiritual and physical, explains the limitations of humans (3.12, 31). They need spiritual birth from above to become sensitive to the divine, to appreciate the spiritual events taking place in Christ, as the story of Nicodemus so clearly shows (3.1-10). This necessitated the incarnation of the Son of God. In him the divine, spiritual, and physical are merged (1.14, 18; 1 Jn 1.1-4; 4.2; 2 Jn 7). If this had not taken place, God would have remained 'unseen'. In Jesus the spiritual becomes visible – he brought the physical and spiritual realities together and made the spiritual accessible to the physical (1.15; 12.49-50; 14.10-11).

2.2.2 Contrasting time: pre-existence, eternity, and earthly time

The Gospel starts with the words: 'In the beginning' (1.1) the Word was and was with God. The Word was there *before* the time of *creation*, and therefore '*pre-existed*'. Although Jesus was apparently not yet '50 years' old according to the crowd, he could say: 'Before Abraham was, I am' (8.57-58). He indeed has an earthly body with which he exists in this world and is bound to the timeframe of this world, but he also has eternal life that is different from the life of this world. Earthly life (Gr. = *psuche*) will end; eternal life (Gr. = *zōe*) will not – it is eternal. Like Jesus, believers, having eternal life, will exist eternally with God – they are moved into the 'timeframe' of God. On this basis Jesus can say, 'even though they die, they will live, and everyone who lives and believes in me will never die' (11.25-26).

2.3 Contrasts with ethical implications: good and evil

God stands in opposition to the devil, not only in his nature, but also in his qualities, actions, and attitude. God gives life through his Son (3.16) while the devil is a murderer from the beginning (8.44). Jesus is true (14.6) while the devil is the father of lies (8.44), etc. Here follows a list of some of the most important ethical contrasts:

(a) The terms:

Life	vs	death (3.15, 16; 5.24; 10.10)
Children of God	vs	children of the devil (8.44; 1 Jn 3.10)
Followers of Jesus	vs	opponents of Jesus (6.66-71; 9.35-41; 1 Jn 2.18-19)
Free from sin	vs	slaves to sin (8.34-38)
Belief in Jesus	vs	unbelief in Jesus (3.15, 16, 36; 5.24; 1 Jn 5.4-5, 10)
Love	vs	hate (3.16, 20; 15.18ff.; 17.14; 1 Jn 2.9, 11; 3.13, 15; 4.20)
Spiritual sight (hear)	vs	spiritual blindness (deaf) (8.47; 9.39-40)
Know God	vs	do not know God (14.17, 20)
Truth	vs	lies (8.44; 14.6; 1 Jn 1.6; 2.21, 27)
Light	vs	darkness (1.5; 3.19; 8.12; 1 Jn 1.5; 2.8)

These contrasts cover different areas, for instance, the form of *existence* (life/death); *identity and status* (free people and contrasting terms), *actions and attitudes* (followers, faith/love and contrasting terms) and *qualitative determination*, namely, being in truth and light, or the opposite. These contrasting qualities are also interrelated, for instance, the person who does what is *true*, comes to the *light* (3.21); he who *believes* has eternal *life* (3.36), and so on.

(b) The theological and ethical implications of these contrasts
An important point for understanding Johannine theology is that qualities like truth, life, knowledge, or even hate, untruthfulness, are not abstract realities existing on their own, as was the case in some ancient philosophies, but are always linked to and expressed by *(P)persons*. Positive or negative qualities are only present and become apparent through people. For instance, qualities like love, life, etc. are present where God or his people are, while murder and lies will be evident where the devil and his people are.

This insight helps us to understand certain central theological issues:

- Through Jesus' *personal* presence, divine qualities like true love, light, truth, or life became present in this world (8.12; 14.6). Where he is, there these qualities are present. He was the *locus* and source of the divine qualities among the people of this world.
- When Jesus became flesh, he did not become bad or evil. Negative or evil qualities are not abstract phenomena, neither do they lurk in the flesh or hide somewhere in creation. No, they are inherent to and exist in persons. When Jesus became flesh, his personal qualities of love, truth, etc. were not separated from him. He still was the truth, life, and light although he became flesh (8.12; 14.6). That is why he identifies himself so clearly in terms of these contrasting qualities by saying, I AM the resurrection and life (11.25), light (8.12), truth (14.6), the one who can set people free (8.36), and so on.

John's message unfolds within a reality typified by both creational and ethical contrasts. This forms a departure point for understanding the message of John. God, who is above, must send his Son to this world to establish his divine qualities in a visible way among people who are in darkness and are slaves of sin.

Schematically the contrasts may be mapped as in Diagram 2.1.

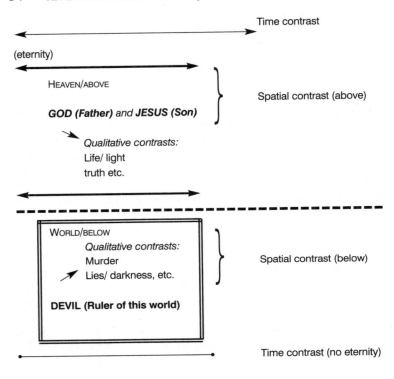

Diagram 2.1

3. God's loving mission to this world: from the 'above' to the 'below'

'For God so loved the world that he gave his only Son, so that everyone who believes in him may not perish but may have eternal life' (3.16) – this verse expresses the centrality of God in John's Gospel. It is he who loves the world and initiates salvation, because he does not want to see people perish.

3.1 Who is the God we meet in the Johannine writings?

There can be no uncertainty who the God is that we meet in John's Gospel – he is the God of the Old Testament, the creator God (1.1-5,

10; 5.26; 6.57) of the Jews (8.41; 8.54; 11.52). He is the God who was active in and through the history of his people (1.6; 3.2; 6.32; 9.3), who was obeyed by Abraham (8.39), and worked through Moses by giving him the Law (1.17; 6.32; 9.29). He was worshipped in the temple in Jerusalem (2.13ff.; 4.20), and was honoured through the cultic activities of the Jews (i.e. purification, Sabbath, feasts – 5.18; 7.22; 9.16). It was him the prophets were speaking about (3.2; 6.45).

The God of Israel is the only true God (3.33; 5.44; 8.26; 17.3). Nobody has ever seen him (1.18; 5.37; 1 Jn 4.12, 20), except for the Son who is close to his Father's heart (1.18). As a living Father, he is the source of life (2.22; 5.26; 6.57; 11.41), of truth (8.40), of protection (10.29; 17.15) as well as the source of, and power behind, all good (9.31-33; see 19.11; 3 Jn 11).

There is, however, one characteristic that particularly typifies God in this Gospel and Letters: This very same God is called 'Father', specifically the Father of Jesus (1.18; 3.35; 5.17, etc.). Through the mediating work of Jesus he reveals himself (14.6-11; 17.6) and becomes the Father of all the followers of Jesus (20.17, see also 8.19, 38, 49; 17.1, 21, 24, 25, etc.).

Theologically this is a crucial point. Jesus does not introduce a new God, only a new revelation of the God of Abraham, Moses and the prophets. He is now the one who makes this God known (1.18). The history of God with his people that started with creation in the Old Testament now continues in and through Jesus.

3.2 The unique relationship between the Father and the Son

A special relationship exists between the Father and the Son. This special and unique relationship goes back to the *pre-existence* of Jesus: the Son was with God, the Father (1.1; 1 Jn 1.2; 2 Jn 3), yes, close to the Father's heart (1.18). He was the only one who has seen the Father (6.46; 1 Jn 4.12). This explains his special and intimate knowledge of the Father (7.28, 29; 8.19, 42), which forms the foundation of his claim to be the one who will make the Father known.

Different expressions are used to describe this unique relationship. There are, for instance, formulas expressing the Father being *in* the Son and vice versa: 'Do you not believe that I am in the Father and the Father is in me?' Jesus asks in 14.10 (the so-called *Immanenzformeln* = formulas of immanence – 8.42; 10.38; 14.20; 17.21-23). Then there are expressions of unity, namely, that the Father and the Son are one (10.30; 17.11, 21, 23; see also 1 Jn 2.23-24), not to mention Jesus' position as the unique Son who is at the Father's side (1.18; 3.16).

However, within this intimate relationship, the difference between Father and Son is always maintained. The Father remains the one who authoritatively sends the Son, while the Son remains the one who is sent (12.49). In Jesus' own words on his return: 'I am going to the Father, because the Father is greater than I' (14.28).

The clearest expression of the unique relationship between the Father and his Son is in the mission of Jesus to this world: God 'so loved the world that he gave his only Son' (3.16). He not only *functionally equipped* his Son, but was also *actively involved* in the execution and *outcome* of the mission.

God, the Father, *functionally equipped* Jesus for his mission. As ancient fathers did when they educated their sons, Jesus' Father showed him everything (5.19-20) and put everything into his hands (3.35; 13.3; 17.2, 7). He gave his Son the authority and power to do whatever he, as Father, did (5.19), *inter alia* to give life and judge (5.19-29; 10.17-18), things that are the prerogative of God alone.

The Father has not only equipped his Son, but also stayed *actively involved* in his mission. God *planned* this mission according to his *will* (6.38-40). This becomes evident in different ways: the Father, for instance, prepared the way for his Son by sending John (the Baptist – 1.6); he determined the schedule for his Son, referred to in the Gospel as 'the hour' (2.4; 7.30; 8.20; 12.27; 13.1; 17.1); he even prepared the symbolic cup of the cross for him to drink (18.11).

The Father did not leave his Son alone but worked through him. Jesus formulates this in 14.10-11 as follows: 'Do you not believe that I am in the Father and the Father is in me? The words that I say to you I do not speak on my own; but the *Father who dwells in me does his works*.' What Jesus does and says are here identified as the works of the Father. His works are continued through the Son (5.22 and 8.15-16; see also 15.1-2). God, the Father, clearly declares himself to be on the side of Jesus. He bears witness to the Son (5.36; 8.18; 1 Jn 5.9), honours, and glorifies him (8.54; 12.28; 17.1, 5).

The Father is also involved with the '*outcome*' of the mission of Jesus. The Father draws those who belong to him to the Son (6.37, 44, 65; 10.29; 17.6). He gives life to those who come to believe (1.12-13; 1 Jn 5.11), loves them (14.21, 23; 16.27; 1 Jn 3.1), protects them (10.29; 17.11ff.), and cares for them (6.32), for instance, by sending the *Paraclete*, the Spirit of truth (14.26; 1 Jn 4.1-3). The children may also ask in prayer according to the will of the Father and the Father will give what they need (15.16; 16.23). However, that is not all: the Father is so intimately involved with his children, that he makes his home with them (14.23), so that they can all be one (17.11, 20-23).

This can all be summarized in the simple understanding that the God of Israel is the Father of Jesus. Through Jesus his master plan for this world unfolds. He sends his Son, Jesus, to make himself known to this world. Through Jesus his words and deeds, his love and grace can be experienced by anybody who believes.

3.3 The Letters enrich the view of God

Although the description of God overlaps largely in the Gospel and Letters, there are also some differences.

The Letters emphasize certain qualities of God even more than the Gospel while others subside into the background. While the concept of God as the one who sent his Son moves into the background in the Letters (see 1 John 4.14; these are typical elements belonging to the narrative of Jesus as it is described in the Gospel), the focus shifts to the qualitative actions of God, like giving life or loving his people. In the Letters God is directly described as light (1 Jn 1.5) and love (1 Jn 4.8, 16), terms implied but not directly linked to God in the Gospel. Strong emphasis also falls on being born of the Father, becoming his children (1 Jn 3.1, 2, 9, 10; 4.2-7; 5.1, 16; etc.) and consequently living a loving life (1 Jn 2.5; 3.17; 4.7ff.). However, the references to the relationship and unity between the Father and the Son that is so prominent in the Gospel (1 Jn 1.2 – pre-existence; 1 Jn 2.1, 22), are not equally found in the Letters.

The reasons for these differences most probably lie in the difference between the situations the Gospel and Letters respectively address. The advantage of having both the Gospel and Letters is that in this way, our theological view is broadened and we can move beyond the restrictions of one single situation or context. Our view of God and indeed many other theological themes are thus enriched.

4. God reaches out – He sends his Son

4.1 A world in need of God – the origin of evil

Before Jesus came, this world, the 'below', was under the power of the 'ruler of this world' (12.31; 14.30; 1 Jn 5.19), and was typified by the presence of darkness, death, and lies. People did not hear the words of God and did not know him (8.19, 54-55; 15.21; 17.25). They were spiritually dead (5.24 by implication) and blind (9.27-41) – reflections of their non-existent relationship with God.

This brings us to the question of the origin of evil. How did it happen that this world, God's creation, ended up in spiritual darkness and slavery? Good, life and truth comes from God. Through the Word all things came into being and he filled them with life and light – but darkness came too (1.1-5). Where did evil and spiritual darkness come from? Two remarks are of some help: In 1 Jn 3.8 the devil is called the one who has sinned from the beginning, forcing the Son to come and destroy the devil's work. In 8.44 the devil is described as the father of lies and a murderer from the beginning – that is where the origin of sin is to be found.

Although the devil is clearly present in the Gospel and Letters, he is not so prominent as in the synoptics. There are, for instance, no exorcisms and Jesus does not meet with the devil in the wilderness. However, some significant things are said about Jesus' opponent, the devil:

(a) The devil is called 'the ruler of this world' (12.31; 14.30; 16.11). This name calls up a specific image, namely that of a ruler with an area which he rules – namely, this world (implying a world of darkness without God). In 1 Jn 5.19 it is said that the whole world actually lies under the power of the evil one. Several things happen to this 'ruler':

(i)   In judgement he is 'cast out' of his domain of rule at the moment Jesus is lifted up on the cross (12.31). This is an expression of complete loss of power. As a 'cast out' person he has no more power or influence over what is happening in this world. Jesus can proceed without any opposition in drawing to him those that belong to him (12.32), since the ruler of this world is already judged (16.7-11). In 1 Jn 3.8 the purpose of the coming of Jesus is described in these terms. He destroys the works of the devil.

(ii)   The power game between Jesus and the devil is extremely one-sided. The ruler of this world has no power over Jesus, as is confirmed in 14.30, where Jesus, in the shadow of the cross, remarks that the ruler of this world is coming. Here we have a hint of the cross as place of conflict between Jesus and the ruler of this world, although this theme is not developed directly. Jesus' victory over evil is consistently emphasized in 1 John (1 Jn 2.13; 4.4; 5.4). Jesus is greater than the ruler of this world and because his people belong to him, they share in his victory (1 Jn 5.4).

(b) References to the influence of the devil in the life of Judas (6.70; 13.2) and other people (8.44), give us some clue about the way the devil is present and active in this world. He works through his children, the slaves of sin (8.34-38).

(i)   Judas is said to be under the influence of the devil (13.2 – the devil has indeed put it into his heart to betray Jesus) and is called a devil himself (6.70). Both by identity, motivation, and action he sides with the devil. What he therefore does when Jesus is arrested (18.2-5) is making the influence of the devil felt. There is also some echo in the Letters of the danger of the devil getting hold of a person, where believers are warned to be on their guard so that the devil cannot touch them (1 Jn 5.18, 21; 2 Jn 8).

(ii)   The crowds who deliver Jesus to the cross are, as the devil's children, also instruments of the devil. In 8.44 the devil is described as the father of lies and a murderer from the beginning. His children will do what their father does (8.41-44; 1 Jn 3.10). When the crowds deliver Jesus, they do so based on a lie – they say he is not the Son of God, although he has told them differently. This makes them liars like their father (see also 1 Jn 2.4; 5.10. see also the references to false prophets in 1 Jn 4.1, 3, 6; 2 Jn 7, 10). They then demand his death and that equates to the act of murder. Jesus himself refers to this act as killing (7.19 hinting at 5.18) and not a lawful execution (as the high priest claims it to be – 19.7). They therefore do as their father does, they murder (8.44; 1 Jn 3.12-15). Indeed, since they come out of this evil world, they listen to the evil world (1 Jn 4.5).

This shows that although the devil as character is not so prominent, his presence is undeniable. Through his children he is present and active. You can detect his influence wherever there is hate, murder, false witness, betrayal and lies, and so forth. It should be noted that this reserved focus on the devil is in line with the rhetorical characteristics of this Gospel. Both 'sides' do not receive equal emphasis. Rather, the emphasis falls on the positive side of the message. Jesus did not come to focus on judgement, but to save the world (3.17; 12.47).

Yes, because God so loved the world, he sent his Son, the Word, to make him known in a world in need of the presence of light and life (1.5-13, 18; 3.16). Through him the light shone in the darkness (1.4-5, 9; 8.12; 12.35-36, 46), and life came to replace death (5.24; 1 Jn 1.2; 4.9). Through the *mission* of Jesus the 'world' was changed forever. This mission is a major motif in the development and structure of the Gospel. It forms the basic framework for Jesus' activities on earth.

4.2 The mission of Jesus

Then Jesus came, the light shone in the darkness (1.4-9) and people got to know God again, by seeing his grace and truth (1.14-17; 8.19; 14.7-11; 15.21-22; 1 Jn 1.1-4; 5.20). Let us now briefly focus on this mission of Jesus.

We have already seen that the mission of the Son is possible because of his unique relationship with the Father, who equipped and sent him. This description of the mission of the Son by the Father is based on the social conventions of ancient mission practices. Sending an envoy to communicate over distances was a basic practice in the ancient world.

What follows is a systematic presentation of the different elements of the mission of the Son in the Gospel. (All the elements of the mission are going to be mentioned here, which might cause some overlap with what was already said about God.) Though the Letters mention the mission (1 Jn 4.14), they do not focus on it at all. In the letters the Father takes centre stage and Jesus is described more in terms of his relation to the presence of the Father.

(1) Prerequisite for the mission: Nobody in this world has seen God or knows him. This asks for something special, namely, revelation from 'above'. To bridge the gap between him and the world through revelation, God decided to send his Son, with whom he stands in a unique relationship (3.16). The Son is in a privileged position. He has seen God and knows him (1.18; 6.46), since he was with the Father (3.11, 13, 31; 7.29; 17.25). He could therefore reveal God, the Father (1.18).

(2) The Sender (Father) prepares his Agent (Son): An agent had to represent the one who sent him. Therefore, the sender first needed to inform his agent what to say or do and to equip him with what was necessary for the mission. Likewise, the Father prepared and equipped the Son for his mission. In 8.28 Jesus claims that he is acting on behalf of the Father since the Father has educated and prepared him. How this happened is described in 5.19-24. The known pattern of education in ancient times, of the father teaching his son what to do, is applied to the relation between the Father and the Son. The Father shows his Son all that he is doing (5.20), and what the Son sees the Father doing, he himself does (5.19). It is a matter of following the example of, or 'copying', the Father. This is what Jesus claims he does: 'the Son can do nothing on his own, but only what he sees the Father doing; for whatever the Father does, the Son does likewise' (5.19) and 'I do nothing on my own, but I speak these things as the Father instructed me ... I always do what is pleasing to him' (8.28-29).

The Father has placed all things in his Son's hands (3.35) and has given him authority over all flesh (17.2). But, what exactly did the Son learn from the Father? Two important things should be noted:

(a) To give *life*: 'Just as the Father raises the dead and gives them life, so also the Son gives life to whomever he wishes' (5.21). Giving life is the prerogative of God alone. However, the Father has given his Son this power (17.2; see also 5.26). Jesus will illustrate this power over life and death when he lays down his life and takes it up again (10.17-18).

(b) To *judge*: 'The Father judges no one but has given all judgement to the Son.' As Jesus claims, 'As I hear, I judge; and my judgement is just, because I seek to do not my own will but the will of him who sent me' (5.22 and 30 respectively). Like giving eternal life, eschatological judgement is also the prerogative of God, the King (3.3, 5; 5.22; cf. also 8.15-16). The Father has also given this task to his Son.

(3) Mission, authority, and purpose: The mission of the Son is clear: he must make the Father known and give eternal life to those who believe (1.18; 12.49-50; 14.6-11; 17.6-8). His authority is derived from the Father who prepared him for that mission and on whose behalf he will act (3.35; 5.30; 8.28; 13.3; 17.2).

(4) Mode of coming: The Father sent the Son into this world (5.23, 36, 37; 6.44, 57; 8.16, 18, 42; 10.36; 11.42; 12.49, etc.). The Son became flesh and dwelt among humans (1.14). As a pre-existent being he now entered into the material world – in him the two worlds (the above and below) coincide. What was unknown and invisible now becomes known and visible through Christ.

5) Performing his mission: The Son obediently executed his mission to please and glorify the Father (8.29; 4.34; 17.4), with the knowledge that the Father will always be with him (8.16; 16.32).

Good agents only did what they were asked to do. They did not act on their own behalf and did not follow their own will. The agent was there to perform a task on behalf of the sender and should therefore take care not to act beyond the boundaries of his commission. In *obedience* the agent must do exactly what the sender required him to do. They should represent and communicate what they had received and had been told by the sender.

In the Gospel Jesus is portrayed as the *ideal Agent*. The Son obediently says and does only what the Father showed and told him to do

(3.11, 32, 34; 5.19; 7.17, 28; 8.26, 28, 38, 40; 9.4; 12.49-50; 14.24; 15.15). He does nothing of his own accord, or on his own authority, but seeks to do the will of the one who has sent him (3.34; 5.30; 6.38; 7.16-18; 8.28-29; 12.49; 14.24, 31; 15.10). Jesus stresses that his teachings and words are simply the teachings and words of the one who has sent him (7.16; 8.28; 14.24).

> **Excursus:** '*I am*'-*sayings* (*Gr.* = *ego eimi*): The Gospel of John is known for the seven 'I am' (*ego eimi*)-*sayings* with predicates (like 6.35; 10.6, 11; 11.25) and several absolute *ego eimi*-sayings (without explicit or implicit predicate – 8.24, 28, 58; 13.19). The *ego eimi*-sayings with predicates include I am ... the bread of life (6.35, 41, 48, 51); the light of life (8.12); the door of the sheepfold (10.7, 9); the good shepherd (10.11, 14); the resurrection and the life (11.25); the way, the truth, and the life (14.7); the true vine (15.1, 5). Usually these sayings (plus the absolute sayings) are linked to either Exod. 3.14, Deut. 32.39, or to the 'I am'-sayings in Deutero-Isaiah (for instance, Isa. 43.10, 25; 45.18-19; 46.4; 48.12, 17; 52.6). Jesus is thus identified as the Lord of history and saviour of Israel. Within these sayings there are allusions to divinity – by using them Jesus implies divine authority. The point is that the 'I am'-sayings may refer to the divine character of Jesus (see the reaction to the words 'I am' in 18.6). Within the context of the mission of Jesus, there might be another aspect to consider, namely recognition and identification of an envoy. The way in which envoys made themselves known at their destinations was to identify themselves with the words 'I am so and so'. On questions like 'who are you' this would also have been the way to answer. Jesus also identifies himself in this world by saying 'I am ...' The predicates like life, light, truth, the good shepherd, etc. are all descriptions that identify him with his divine origin. This intensifies the divine undertones of the words 'I am'. The words 'I am' therefore identify Jesus not only as a divine agent or envoy, but also as a divine person.

(6) Returning to the original location after completing the task: After completion of a mission, an agent returned to the sender. The mission of Jesus also followed this pattern. He returns to the Father (8.14), to the 'above' where he came from (7.33-36; 8.21-23). The cross-events mark this point of Jesus' return to the glory he had before he was sent (17.5). That is why his last words on the cross could be, 'It is finished' (19.28-30), indicating that his mission is completed. He has done what he was sent for (17.4-5). He came from heaven, completed his work and returned to heaven (3.13; 6.62; 8.14) where his Father is (7.33; 13.1, 3; 14.28; 16.5, 28; 17.11, 13; 20.17).

(7) The results of the mission and the report back of the Agent to the Sender: It was an ancient practice that after the completion of a mission, the agent reported back on what he had done, what happened, and what should be done in future. This is understandable, since the agent was *inter alia* the eyes and ears of the sender during the mission. He

must therefore help the sender to get up to date with the outcome of the mission.

Again, Jesus' mission follows this pattern. He reports back to his Father in the prayer in chapter 17. He has completed his mission with success (17.1-5). As a result of his mission, the family of God was established in this world (17.6-8). However, what will happen to them now that he returns to the Father? Jesus asks the Father to protect and equip them for their task in this world (17.9-19). Jesus also prays for those who will still become believers in future through the mission work of the original believers (17.20-23). Yes, the mission will have to continue, through the believers (14.12; 17.18; 20.21; 21.1ff.). They will have the help of a special Helper (14.16-17), the Spirit, and will be under the protection of the Father (17.15). He also prays for the distant future – he asks that the believers could be where he is! (17.24).

God so loved the world that he sent his unique Son (3.16). And this mission was a success! Schematically the mission may be presented as in Diagram 2.2:

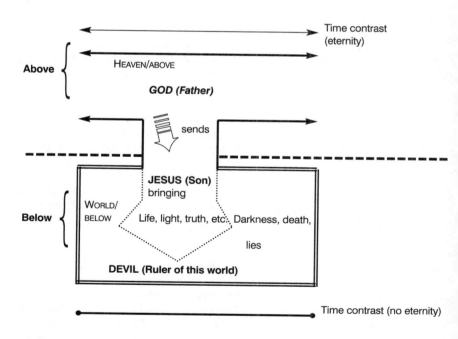

Diagram 2.2

It would be worthwhile to get to know this Agent, the Son of God, a little better.

5. Get to know Jesus better (Christology)

John's Gospel was written so that people may believe *that Jesus is the Christ, the Son of God* (20.31). It is thus little wonder that we find so much emphasis on the identity and nature of Jesus in the Gospel: who is he? (5.12), where is he? (7.11), where is he going? (7.35), is he bigger than Abraham? (8.53), and so on. The Gospel provides the answers.

The Johannine view of Jesus (Christology) is developed in many different ways:

- Jesus is given *names* of significance, like the Word, King of Israel or Son of Man.
- He is described figuratively by means of *imagery* like the true vine (15.1ff.) or good shepherd (10.1ff.).
- He talks about himself as is evident in the 'I am'-*sayings* (Gr. = *ego eimi* – 6.35; 8.12, etc.).
- He *preaches*/talks to individuals like Nicodemus or to the crowds and informs them about his mission. Stylistic features like forensic language (5.31ff.; 8.12ff.) or misunderstandings give Jesus a chance of elaborating on his message (3.3ff.).
- *Others talk* about him, like the healed man (chapter 9), or even confess him, like Thomas (20.28).
- He does *signs* like turning water into wine to illustrate that he is the eschatological bridegroom; he cleanses the temple to draw attention to himself as the new eschatological temple (chapter 2), etc.

Drawing from this variety of Christological evidence a complex picture of Jesus Christ emerges. Let us briefly survey some of the most important aspects of the person of Jesus.

5.1 Jesus has many names … names with a message

Jesus has many significant names – names like King of Israel, Son of God, Messiah, Lamb of God, the Holy One of God, God, to name but a few. These are not just names, but are titles that tell us more about Jesus. It is like calling somebody a 'General' today – it immediately tells you where he works (in the army), what his status is (the highest), his relative income (higher than the rest of the army), and so on.

Just look at some of the names in the impressive list we find in chapter 1 alone: Lord (YHWH of the Old Testament – 1.23), Lamb of God (the one who will get rid of sin – 1.29, 36); Son of God (standing in a special relation to the Father – 1.34, 49); Rabbi (teacher) (the one who teaches and reveals – 1.38, 49); Messiah (Christ) (kingly ruler who would save God's people – 1.41); Jesus of Nazareth (a local Jew – 1.45); King of Israel (the One who will rule the eschatological Israel – 1.49); Son of man (the eschatological judge – 1.51; see also 1.27, 30, 33, 45). And these are not the only names used of Jesus in the Gospel. Names like prophet (4.19), Holy one of God (6.69), 'I am' (10.11), or Saviour of the world (4.42), could also be added. Most of these names used of Jesus also have 'histories' behind them (like Messiah, Son of God, Son of Man, Lord). They have some past (Old Testament) significance which is then projected onto Jesus to express his significance. In doing this John makes sure that his readers realize that the significance of Jesus by far surpasses the significance of all these religious figures.

5.2 Jesus' identity as the Son of God, the Father

Although so many names are used of Jesus, a significant title for Jesus is *Son* (1.34; 1 Jn 1.3; 5.5, 20; 2 Jn 3). In spite of finer nuances, the use of the phrases Son, Son of God, and Son of man overlap significantly, and often there is no real difference in meaning. There is a good reason why the 'Father–Son' language is so important. It recalls the most intimate social grouping of ancient times, namely, the family, and expresses the intimate relationship between the Father and Son in these terms.

The family history of the Son goes back to before creation when he was with his Father (1.1; 8.58; 17.5, 24; 1 Jn 2.13, 14). The fact that the Son created the world confirms that he pre-existed creation. He 'predates' the important figures in the Old Testament (Abraham – 8.58; Isaiah – 12.41), while Old Testament prophets and the scriptures knew about him. Moses wrote about him (1.45), scripture witnesses about him (5.39; 19.36-37; 1 Jn 2.22; 5.1).

The significance of these references to Old Testament figures is of course that Jesus is not bringing a new or different religion, but stands in continuation with the history of the creator God of Israel (1.2-3). He does not reveal any god but the true and only God (17.3), initially worshipped in Jerusalem, but now worshipped in Spirit and truth (4.24). This God is his Father with whom he stands in an intimate relationship.

Jesus is called the *unique* (Gr. = *monogenēs*) Son of the Father – there is no other like him (1.14, 18; 3.16, 18) and never will be. Nobody has ever seen (= intimately known) God (1.18), except Jesus who was in the bosom of the Father and knows him intimately (1.18; 7.29; 8.54-55; 17.25-26). This intimate relationship puts Jesus in the position of being able to make the Father known (1.18; 14.7; 17.25-26). He not only has first-hand knowledge of the Father but the Father has also empowered him to reveal him to this world (3.35; 17.2). This is the argument of the healed man in chapter 9 too: if Jesus were not from God, he could do nothing. On this basis the Father and the Son are described as 'one' (10.30).

5.3 Jesus' humanity and divinity

In 1 Jn 1.1-4 it is stated that Jesus was seen, heard and touched by his disciples, but was also the Word of life that was with the Father. In the Prologue of the Gospel both the human and divine sides of Jesus are expressed – He is called God, but also became flesh and dwelt among his people (1.1-18). This relationship between the humanity and divinity of Jesus is one of the focal points of research and discussion in Johannine Christology. What is the relationship between the human and the divine in Jesus?

5.3.1 Jesus is God

Jesus is explicitly called 'God' (Gr. = *theos*) at the beginning and end of the Gospel. The Gospel starts by explicitly saying: 'The Word was God' (1.1; see 1.18; 1 Jn 5.20). It concludes with Thomas confessing the risen Jesus as 'My Lord and my God' (20.28).

However, 1.1 does not only state that Jesus *was* God, but also that he *was with* (Gr. = *pros*) God, suggesting not only identification, but also distinctiveness (see 1.18 where the Son – God – is at the heart of God, the Father). Jesus was God, but simultaneously he was orientated towards and indeed with God. This becomes the challenging enigma of John's Gospel – 'God and also with God'.

That Jesus is confessed as the pre-existent Word, that was God (1.1), is undeniably part of the message of the Gospel. That is why Jesus can be identified through qualities associated with the divine, namely, truth and life (14.6; 1 Jn 1.2-3; 5.20), resurrection (11.25-26) or light (8.12), righteousness and love (1 Jn 3.7, 16). But that he is also distinct from God, the Father, is emphasized equally (1.1, 18).

Jesus' divinity was not apparent from his physical appearance as a human, but when he acted and spoke, it became clear that he was 'from

God'. As Bultmann said, the glory of God was hidden within the earthly person of Jesus. However, people needed special spiritual vision to be able to recognize that in this physical Jesus there is a divine presence. This is the point the healed blind man made (9.24-41). He argued that if God was not with Jesus empowering him in a special way, Jesus would not have been able to do the miraculous things he had done. The way Jesus' divinity therefore becomes apparent is through his deeds (see also 6.63; 8.16; 10.37f.; 14.8-11). The Pharisees fail to see or recognize this, because they are spiritually blind. They therefore saw the man Jesus, but not the Son of God.

The debate about the exact nature of the divinity and humanity of Jesus is an ongoing one. It cannot be treated in detail here, but the following excursus should give some indication of what makes up the essence of this critical debate.

Excursus: *Jesus as God*: One of the mysteries of this Gospel is how to understand the designation of Jesus as 'God' within a monotheistic society without implying ditheism? The challenge for the early Christians indeed was how their faith in Jesus could be synchronized with their faith in the Father without endangering the uniqueness of God nor the uniqueness of Jesus within the confines of monotheism. Only a few of the many attempts to explain this mystery will be treated in order to gain some insight into the debate.

• One effort interprets the relation between the Father and Son within the experiences of the original community (Theobald). It is pointed out that Jesus does not call himself God, but the narrator and Thomas do so in the form of confessions (1.1, 18; 20.28). The Gospel, therefore, reflects the well-formulated answer of the Johannine community to the accusations of ditheism after separation from the synagogue. In answer to the Jewish opponents who understood the claims of Jesus as implying deism (5.18; 10.33; 19.7), the community emphasized the mission of Jesus on behalf of the Father. The Father sent him (5.23, 37; 6.44, etc.) and he does nothing on his own. His authority is based on, and embedded in, the authority of the Father. Jesus did not challenge the position of the only God. However, Jesus acts through the Spirit and the presence of the Spirit identifies him with God; and as the wisdom of God, Jesus is the source of the Spirit. This position would have neutralized the accusations of the Jews.

• Another perspective turns to the socio-philosophical ecology of the world within which the Gospel originated. In Philo, the *Wisdom of Solomon*, and some other early Jewish literature there is evidence that Jewish monotheism was not understood too rigidly. Since the third or second century BCE, even in Jewish circles, there were speculations about a second 'presence' or godly figure (although not in the form of a human person). A highest angel, for instance, came into question, as is apparent in the vision in Ezekiel about Moses who was put on the throne of God, receiving a crown and staff with all the heavenly powers bowing before him (Van der Horst). Enoch receives similar divine tokens and is even called 'small YHWH' (3 Enoch). This might form the background for considering the divine nature of Jesus; since he is not ontologically equated to God, the Father, nevertheless stands in close relation to him.

> • Others refer to different usages of the word 'god' to solve the mystery. In the Greek literature prior to the New Testament the term 'god' (Gr. = *theos*) was commonly used for a variety of mythical figures, abstract powers, and even people with exceptional abilities like Plato, or politicians like Lentulus. Even Jewish writers (see the LXX, Philo, *Jubilees*, Qumran literature, etc.) used the term god in such a variety of meanings. The term was *inter alia* used to indicate a *close relationship* of somebody, even a human, with God, the Father. This echoes Jesus' argument in 10.33-38, where even humans are called 'gods'. The point seems to be that the word 'god' could also be used in a broader sense than strictly referring to the one monotheistic God. Thus the use of the term 'god' is broadened to include the Son of God, who may now be called 'God' because of his close relationship with the Father. He performed divine deeds and thus 'earned' the honour of being confessed as 'Lord and God'. In this way monotheism is honoured (there are not gods) and the unity and diversity between Father and Son are maintained.

5.3.2 Jesus was truly human

Jesus is not only God. He also became human. He became flesh and dwelt among people on earth. The image of 1.14 is that of Jesus pitching his tent among humans on earth – like God once appeared in truth and grace in a tent, the tabernacle. God came to dwell among his people, and this time as a human who could be heard, seen and touched (1 Jn 1.1-2).

The question however is: how human was Jesus really? This question is significant since it seems that the opponents, the antichrists in 1 Jn 2.22; 4.2-3, thought that Jesus was not truly human – he only appeared to be human (this view is called docetism). Even some modern-day scholars argue that Jesus is described in such heavenly language that it is difficult to believe that he was human (Käsemann).

The humanity of Jesus is attested to in different ways (1.14; 1 Jn 4.1-2; 2 Jn 7).

(a)   He displayed normal *human characteristics*: he was wearied from his journey (4.6); his soul could be troubled and he even cried (12.27; 13.21; 11.35); he became hungry and thirsty and ate and drank (19.28; per implication 2.1ff.; 4.7-8; 6.1ff.; 13.21ff.; 21.9ff.).

(b)   He had a *physical human body* of flesh and blood (6.51, 55; 19.34; 1 Jn 5.8); he was seen and heard and touched as human by his compatriots without indication that he was anything different (5.18; 7.27; 8.57; 10.33; 1 Jn 1.1-3). He was scourged as human (19.1ff.; 19.5), physically died (19.33), and was buried according to the normal procedures (19.39ff.).

(c)   There is no indication anywhere in the Gospel that on a physical level people recognized him as being different or special. He was part of a *human family* with a mother and father (1.45; 2.1, 3, 12;

6.42; 19.26), as well as brothers (2.12; 7.3, 10). He was indeed identified as Jesus of Nazareth, son of Joseph (1.45). His brothers treat him as one of them and do not even believe in him (7.5).

Exactly because Jesus was simultaneously divine and human, he could represent God in a visible and concrete way among humans. In him the divine and human met in a unique way.

5.4 Jesus, the Revealer

As was already said, the activities of Jesus unfold within the framework of his *mission*. What was already said about the mission is not going to be repeated here, but it should be noted that Jesus as revealing Agent of God is indeed central to the understanding of who Jesus is. He, the Son of God, was sent by the Father. He became flesh, and revealed the Father to those who believed (1.18; 17.6-8). Several titles identify Jesus as the one who *reveals*. He is, for instance, called the Word (1.1), prophet (1.21, 25; 4.19; 6.14; 7.40, 52; 9.17), Rabbi or teacher (1.38, 49; 3.2; 4.31; 6.25; 9.2; 11.8, 28; 13.13, 14; 20.16), and the 'way' to salvation and God (10.7-10; 14.6ff.)

(a) The first title used for Jesus is 'the *Word*' (Gr. = *logos*; 1.1). In the ancient world the word *logos* was often used as a description for a mediatory figure, the one who is responsible for the communication between the transcendent reality and earthly world. The word is used in a similar way in 1.1-2. Jesus became flesh to reveal the divine qualities of truth and grace, since he came to make the Father known (1.14-18; see also 1 Jn 1.1). The first Letter specifically draws attention to the revelation of Jesus through his physical presence. The disciples could hear, see and touch him, but they also realized that he is the *Word of Life* – he is the one who not only reveals, but also brings eternal life to them (1 Jn 1.1-3). Revelation of life and love came in and through the Son whom they could listen to and even touch.

(b) Jesus is also called *prophet*, in other words, a person sent with a message from God. What he says is true and his revelation can be believed. The Samaritan woman is the first one to identify Jesus as a prophet, since he had foreknowledge of her personal life (4.19) – what he said was true (see also 7.40). The blind man in chapter 9 had the same experience. Jesus told him to wash in the pool of Siloam. He did that and could see. It was enough proof for him that Jesus was a prophet (9.17). Not only the words, but also the deeds of Jesus convinced the crowds that Jesus was a prophet. They experienced the power of God in him (6.14). He was from God and could therefore speak on behalf of God.

(c)   Another popular title referring to Jesus' revelatory work is *Rabbi* or *teacher*. His followers predominantly use these titles, indicating Jesus' superior knowledge with which he teaches them to be proper children of God. (See also 1 Jn 5.20.)

(d)   The revelatory work of Jesus is also expressed through imagery. Jesus is the 'way' to the Father. Whoever knows him knows the Father (14.6ff.). By listening to his words and looking at his deeds, the Father becomes present among the disciples, since Jesus functionally reveals God to them (14.9-11).

5.5 Jesus, the King

The coming of the kingdom of God is central to the message of the synoptic Gospels (Mark 1.15 *par.*). In the Gospel of John, Jesus is also portrayed as king, but with a significantly lower frequency. The concept of the kingdom of God (mentioned in 3.3, 5) is substituted by the familial concept of eternal life (3.15-16) as the major way to express salvation.

There are some references to Jesus as a king or Messiah (= Christ) in the initial parts of the Gospel (1.41, 49; 4.25, 29; 7.26, 41; 9.22; 10.24; 11.27; 12.34; 20.31; 1 Jn 2.1; 2.22; 4.2; 5.1; 2 Jn 3, 7). Nathanael is the first one to call Jesus 'King of Israel' (1.49). This idea is later echoed by the crowds who wanted to make Jesus king (6.15). The crowds in Jerusalem also welcomed him as King of Israel (12.13-15).

It is, however, at the crucifixion scene that Jesus' kingship emerges as a major theme. His powerful actions when the soldiers came to arrest him illustrate his kingly power and mastery over the situation (18.1-10). Jesus is in complete control, since he has received power from above (19.11). The events of the cross are indeed the enthronement scene of Jesus, the Messiah, the King of the Jews. His title on the cross announces this. It said: 'King of the Jews'. This title was written as the verdict of the earthly judge, Pilate and reflects Jesus' discussion with Pilate about the kingdom. Jesus clearly told Pilate that he was king, not of a kingdom of this world, but from above (18.36-37). Jesus was truly the Messiah who came to establish the kingdom, not of this world, but of the world of God.

5.6 The added symphony of the Letters

The description of Jesus in the Gospel and Letters overlaps in many ways – he is the Son, the Christ who is pre-existent; he overpowered evil and brought life, and so on. The Letters, however, add one or two notes to this Christological symphony. The salvific work of Jesus is described in more traditional terms than in the Gospel: Jesus' *blood* cleanses people from all sin (1 Jn 1.7); yes, Jesus is the *propitiation* for our sins (1 Jn 2.2; 4.10). Such sacrificial language is not found in the Gospel. In this context Jesus is also called the 'advocate' for our defence (Gr. = *paraklētos*; 1 Jn 2.1), a name that is used for the Spirit in the Gospel (chapters 14–16). Certain qualities of Jesus, like his sinlessness (1 Jn 3.5), his purity (1 Jn 3.3), or his righteousness (1 Jn 2.1, 29) also receive special mention in the first Letter.

5.7 Conclusion

Christology dominates the message of the Gospel, and it is a functional Christology – we do not only get to know Jesus through his titles, but also through his actions and revelatory words. The Gospel is not just about defending the person of Jesus against the attacks of his Jewish opponents (apologetic), but also about expressing the existential difference Jesus made by revealing the unseen God and establishing eternal relations between him and his children (soteriological and kerygmatic). All relationships with God are and should be defined in terms of the relationship with Jesus. Jesus is the one sent by the Father to make him known.

6. Salvation: becoming part of the family of God

Jesus was sent on a mission to save the world (4.42; 1 Jn 4.14), but what is supposed to happen? What is salvation? The purpose of Jesus' mission is echoed in 20.31 or 1 Jn 5.13 where it is stated that Jesus brings eternal life to those who believe. Yes, a person receives eternal life through *faith in Jesus* and *spiritual birth*, as 1.12-13 states: 'Yet to all who received him, to those who *believed* in his name, he gave the right to become children of God – children ... *born* of God' (see 1 Jn 5.11-13).

6.1 The way to salvation: believe in Jesus

6.1.1 The problem – it is a matter of existence

Why is salvation necessary? For what reason should Jesus save people? The answer is obvious, from sin. But what is sin according to the Gospel? The essence of sin in the Gospel is not necessarily doing wrong things, but doing THE wrong thing, that is, not accepting Jesus as the Christ, the Son of God (16.9). Not believing in him excludes a person from everything Jesus has to offer … eternal life, membership in the family of God, real love, truth and light, and so on. In 6.29 Jesus says to the crowd: 'This is the work of God, that you believe in him whom he sent.' Not accepting Jesus, implies that you side with his opponent, the devil (8.42-47) and that is the major sin. Such a person is spiritually dead.

One should therefore not confuse the symptoms with the real problem. The real issue is the refusal to accept Christ, and such refusal results in evil behaviour that became physically visible in hate, murder (3.20; 8.44; 15.18ff.), lies (8.44), theft (12.6), or seeking self-honour (5.44; 15.19), loving this world and not God (1 Jn 2.15-17; see also 3.19-20; 5.42). Such deeds are only symptomatic of the state of existence of a person without God. Believing in Jesus will cure this 'disease' and the symptoms will be treated automatically – that person will pass from death to life, from lies to truth (5.24) and that will become apparent in his deeds.

Well, there seems to be a logical problem here and perhaps even a circular argument. Jesus was sent to save … if you reject him you sin and are therefore in need of salvation. But if he did not come, this problem would not have arisen and salvation would not have been necessary, or so it seems.

The author of the Gospel is thoroughly aware of this problem. In 15.22 he makes the following remark: 'If I had not come and spoken to them, they would not have sin; but now they have no excuse for their sin.' This echoes his remark to the Pharisees in 9.41: 'If you were blind, you would not have sin. But now that you say, "We see," your sin remains.' A few remarks should put this in proper perspective.

There seems to be no uncertainty about the fact that the world is in darkness and does not know God; even more, they hate God, as is stated in 15.21 and 23, the immediate context of 15.22. They are not in a 'saved state' and do not even realize it: they *think* they see, as 9.41 states, but actually, they are blind. And because they deceive themselves in such a way, they do not even look for the truth around them. They argue with the blind man and reject him, even though the blind man clearly tells them the truth (9.24-34). They have no realization of the state they are in. God however knows that they are blind and in total darkness without any relationship with him. They are children of the prince of this world (8.44). The fact that they do not realize how blind they are does not suddenly exempt them from all guilt and turn their relationship with God from non-existent to a perfect relationship. No, even though they do not realize they are blind, they are still guilty of being blind and without God – they will never experience God's eternal life. They are not suddenly saved – that is, standing in a perfect relation to God – just because they are ignorant of God. No, they need Jesus Christ to restore their relationship with God. Between brackets: from a dogmatic point of view, one can argue that if you do not know of your sin (you are blind) you should not be held responsible for your deeds. John does not argue this way. It is not the deeds that count but the lack of a *relationship* with God. And a lack of a relationship with God is not restored by being ignorant of God. If you do not have this relationship, you are not with God and are therefore in need of restoration of your relationship with him, or else you would simply die without that relationship.

That is why a loving God sent his Son to open the eyes of people (chapter 9) and to be the light of life to this world (8.12). The moment the light came into this world, darkness and blindness, yes, the lack of knowledge of God, stood in sharp contrast to the light and knowledge of God. Nobody could now claim that he or she does not know something like light or does not know the presence of God among them. Neither could they argue that they are on the side of God when they explicitly place themselves in opposition to Jesus. They have heard the words of God and those words will judge them (12.48) – there are no excuses any longer.

Let us now look at how salvation – establishing the relationship between God and people – works through *faith* that leads to spiritual *birth*.

6.1.2 Faith as a means of attaining salvation
Faith is not defined in a single verse in the Gospel, but its full extent is gradually developed throughout the Gospel. A complicating factor is that the word faith is used for different meanings in the Gospel. Not all faith is salvific faith, for instance, the 'believers' in 6.60-66 or in 8.31 (see 8.44) are apparently not saved. Let us briefly investigate a few contexts where faith does *not* lead to salvation to see what went wrong, and then come to a proper description of salvific faith.

(a) Faith for the wrong reasons: Faith that accepts Jesus, but for the wrong reasons and without an adequate change in one's attitude

towards oneself or towards Jesus does not seem to be salvific, even though a positive attitude towards Jesus is expressed. Consider the following examples.

There are people who believed in Jesus' name because they saw the *miraculous signs* he performed (2.22-25). Jesus' reaction to them was not all that positive: 'But Jesus would not entrust himself to them, for he knew all men' (2.24). It seems that the inadequacy of faith based on signs alone is emphasized. Although this positive attitude might be the 'first step' towards Jesus, it does not ensure salvation yet. Believing in Jesus as miracle worker is not enough.

Certain people seem to follow Jesus simply for the sake of the gifts and benefits they could receive (6.14-15, 25-27). Where such a *self-seeking attitude* is linked to faith, such faith seems to be inadequate. There is another example of believers (they are even called *disciples*) who are not willing to follow Jesus *unconditionally* (6.66), because his teachings are too difficult for them (6.60). They decided to turn home, which counts for a decision against Jesus (6.66). A self-seeking attitude that prevents a full and unconditional confession like that of Peter, backed by staying with Jesus when others leave (6.68-69), indeed hinders faith from being salvific. The danger of such a self-seeking attitude is reiterated in a different way in 12.42-43, where people who seemingly believe, do not want to confess Jesus openly, since 'they loved praise from men more than praise from God' (12.43). They were afraid of being thrown out of the synagogue and this prevented them from openly confirming their faith.

(b) Faith that is not expressed in deeds: Jesus' argument in 8.30-47 emphasizes that faith without resulting deeds is inadequate. According to 8.30 many put their faith in him, even as he spoke (8.30). Jesus explains to these *believers* (8.31) that being a child of God should become apparent in their behaviour (8.39-42). Although these people 'believe' (8.31), their deeds deny such belief, proving them to belong to the family of Satan (8.44). Salvation eludes them, since you cannot believe one thing and do something else.

(c) True faith involves acceptance and deeds: Jesus physically and spiritually heals a blind man in chapter 9. This blind man concludes that Jesus must be from God (9.27-33), and defends his conviction to the point of losing everything (9.34). But there is a twist in the story. Even though the man is willing to lose everything in defending Jesus, he is not saved yet, not before he also accepts Jesus for who he really is, the Lord, the Son of man (9.35-38). It becomes clear: acceptance of Jesus without works is not adequate, neither are works without acceptance.

Active, self-sacrificing defence of Jesus, because of a conviction that he is from God, and a consequent full acceptance of his divine identity to the point of worship (9.38) imply salvation. Intellectual acceptance of Jesus and concrete, existential behaviour resulting from that go hand in hand when it comes to salvation.

In a nutshell: salvific faith is a self-sacrificing, intellectual and existential acceptance of the message and person of Jesus to the extent that it completely transforms a person's thoughts and deeds in accordance with Jesus' message and leads to an obedient life of doing what a child of God should do.

An important remark remains to be made: It should also be noted that faith alone *is* not yet salvation. It is the means of attaining salvation. It opens the person up towards Jesus, the source of salvation, the Giver of eternal life. This also applies to the Letters, although the focus is more on the acceptance of the authority of Jesus and his message (1 Jn 3.23; 5.1, 5, 10, 13; not in 2–3 John). Birth from above is still needed.

6.1.3 Salvation: being born into the family of God

Those who *believe* receive eternal life, because they are *born* of God (1.12-13; 3.3, 5; 1 Jn 5.1-5). Being born as a child of God (1.12-13) enables such a person to participate as a spiritual being in the spiritual reality of God (3.1-16 et al.; 1 Jn 2.29). This is the moment of salvation.

In ancient families birth was a defining social event, since it determined the family (Gr. = *oikos*) a person belonged to and therefore also his social stratification. It was further believed that a person's character and personality were given to him *via* the seed of his father and was augmented by education and other circumstances. These conditions also determined the expected behaviour of that person (8.31ff.; 1 Jn 2.29; 3.9-10).

These social convictions underline the importance of the birth language in the Gospel and Letters. In 1.13 it is stated that children of God are born 'out of (Gr. = *ek*) God'. In 1 Jn 3.9 it is put even sharper: 'No one born of God commits sin; for God's nature (= seed – Gr. = *sperma*) abides in him, and he cannot sin because he is born of God.' Persons born of (the seed of) God are not only given the ability to partake in the divine reality of God, but are also born with the divine characteristics in them, much like those that an ordinary baby receives from his father through birth. This does not imply that believers become divine or become gods, but it does imply that believers carry the characteristics of God in them. They, for instance, have eternal life (1 Jn 5.11), they are sons of light (12.36) who act in the light (1 Jn 1.7), the truth abides in them (2 Jn 2) and they follow the truth (3 Jn 3-4).

Excursus: *The role of the cross in salvation:* The cross-events function as an important motif in the Gospel and Letters, although there were efforts to devalue the role of the cross in John's literature, especially in comparison to the Pauline 'theology of the cross', where the atoning and reconciliatory values of the cross are emphasized.

There are different reasons for the cross in the Johannine literature, each of these opens up a different perspective. The cross serves, for instance, as the moment of the enthronement of Jesus (his title on the cross is 'King of the Jews'), illustrating his kingship (18–20). It underlines his righteousness and divine nature of service (16.10; 13.1ff., see also 1.29) as well as his power of judgement (12.31; 14.30; 16.11). It shows that the life of Jesus, including the events of the cross, are determined by divine design (eschatological plan), with divine love as the deepest motivation for the cross (3.16). However, two aspects are of special importance, the cross as *locus* of *revelation* and the question of whether the cross has an *atoning function*.

(i) The death of Jesus as revelation. Salvation comes about when a person believes in Jesus and is reborn. It is therefore of extreme importance that a person should be able to recognize Jesus for who he is, or else he will not believe and will consequently not be saved. The cross-events serve this purpose, as is illustrated in the story of the unbelieving Thomas. When he sees the resurrected Jesus, he can only confess: 'My Lord and my God', identifying the divinity of Jesus (20.28). That is why Jesus could say: 'When you lift up (crucify) the Son of Man, then *you will know that I am*' (8.28). The cross-events do not only reveal that Jesus is the resurrection and life (11.25-26), because he has power over life and death (10.17-18) but also that God is with him (16.32). The unique relationship between the Father and Son, as well as the presence of the Father with the Son, are revealed through the cross-events (16.27ff.; 17.7, 25; 14.18-21). This defines and reveals the divine identity of Jesus. That is why the cross is not pictured as Jesus' passion, but is consistently labelled as his *glorification* (7.39; 12.16, 23; 13.31, 32; 17.1, 5). When Jesus asks his Father to glorify him on the cross, he actually asks of the Father to make his true identity and status visibly known to people (7.39; 8.54; 11.4; 12.16, 23, 28; 13.31-32). Through those events people will recognize him for who he is, and will glorify him.

(ii) Is the death of Jesus atoning? The question whether the death of Jesus is an act of atonement in the thinking of John is significant because of the importance of atonement in the rest of the New Testament. A problem scholars have with the cross-events in the *Gospel* is the complete lack of references to the blood, expiation, or propitiation that are so common in, for instance, the Pauline literature. This caused some to brand the cross-theology of John as bloodless and without any idea of atonement or propitiation.

A common argument against the view that the Gospel lacks atonement language is that atoning undertones might be present in the expression that the 'Lamb of God takes away the sin of this world' (1.29, 36), but this is not convincing. No consensus exists among scholars on the interpretation of this expression. Whether John has the Paschal lamb in mind (that was never an atoning lamb, but symbolizes God's protection), or perhaps a more generic view of lambs that are sacrificed, is not a certainty.

The reason for the lack of atonement or blood language in the Gospel may probably be found in the reason for writing the Gospel. The soteriology of this Gospel is not formulated in an abstract, a-historical way. The Gospel was written in a situation of conflict between Johannine Christians and the disciples of Moses (the synagogue Jews) who did not want to recognize Jesus for who he was, although they did not see it that way (see the discussion between Jesus and the disciples of Moses in 9.38-41). John's aim was to emphasize that Jesus is the One who reveals the true presence of God. He is the only way to salvation, against other solutions offered by the opponents. As a result John focused on the revelatory nature of Jesus rather than on his atoning treatment of individual sins. This does not imply that John would address the issue of salvation in this fashion in every situation. As becomes clear in 1 John, he does not hesitate to refer to the *blood* of Jesus that *purifies* from every sin (1 Jn 1.7), or to refer to the loving God who sent his Son as an atoning sacrifice/propitiation (Gr. = *hilasmos*) for our sins (1 Jn 4.10; see also 1 Jn 2.2).

These atoning expressions in 1 John refer to a different situation, dealing with an inner-communal situation where the questions about personal sin (wrong deeds and a broken relation between the individual and God) are addressed. A different situation – the problem of guilt before God and individual sin – requires a different approach (blood that cleanses and the need for propitiation). It would therefore be wrong to conclude from the Gospel that according to John there is no blood-theology or expiation. The Letters show that where the situation prompts these questions, John confirms the cleansing function of the blood of Jesus as well as his propitiation for sins.

6.2 Being saved: having eternal life or being a child in the family of God

Being born into the family of God through faith in Jesus implies a new identity, new social relations and new status. Believers now have eternal life. What happens to the believer is now developed in analogy to an earthly child in his family. What is true of a child in an ordinary family is figuratively applied to the child of God in his heavenly family. As a child is born into an earthly family, the child of God is born into a heavenly family. As the father of an earthly family feeds and protects his children, the heavenly Father will feed and protect his children, obviously in a spiritual way. As a child should obey the teachings of his father, a child of God should obey the words of God. The author of John therefore uses the characteristics of an ordinary family as an analogy to explain what happens to a person who believes in Jesus and becomes part of the people of God.

The existence of the child of God, being born of God, is now determined by the rules and dynamics of this new divine family he or she became part of. These children of God have a new Father and therefore they will behave differently, since they must now obey their Father (8.38, 42; 1 Jn 3.8-10). Although the believers are not taken out of their physical communities or families – Jesus still talks to his earthly brothers (7.1ff.) and still take cares of his mother (19.26-27) – another family, namely, the figurative family of God, now determines their lives and behaviour (20.17). Eternal life opens up the opportunity for a person to exist and participate in, and be part of the divine family of God, although he is still part of his earthly family – and it is not a matter of split loyalty. All loyalty should belong to the family of God. Within the confines of this new social reality, the family of God, believers could act (8.34ff.), and enter into relations (13.34-35; 15.9-18), having fellowship (1 Jn 1.3-4), experiencing the heavenly reality in the form of peace and love (14.23, 27; 1 Jn 4.7ff.; 5.1ff.), and so on.

Eternal life is indeed a religious and not a biological term, since it expresses the existential reality of a person entering into a relationship with God. In most of the usages in John's Gospel the term 'eternal life' may be substituted by 'to be in/receive a state of being which allows participation (actions and relations) in the divine reality of and with God' (i.e. 5.40). This new life is expressed on different levels that will receive attention now.

6.2.1 Life (salvation) means an intimate relationship with the Father and the Son

A basic characteristic of a child of God is *knowing* the Father and the Son (17.3; 1 Jn 3.1; 4.7). This is not only cognitive knowledge but *relational knowledge*, resulting from the intimate relationship between the believer, the Father and the Son. Because you are so intimately involved with the other person, you get to know him well. This intimate relationship between the believer and Jesus is aptly expressed in the image of the true vine (15.1-8). The intimacy between Jesus and the believer, resembling that of a branch in a vine (15.1-8), forms the essence of a fruitful life that honours God. This intimate relationship is essential, since if believers do not abide in Jesus (15.4; 1 Jn 3.24), they cannot bear any fruit (1 Jn 2.28). This 'abiding in Christ' is concretely expressed through concepts like remaining in Jesus' words (14.23; 15.7; 1 Jn 2.4-5), keeping his commandments (1 Jn 2.3-5), abiding in his love (15.10, 17; 1 Jn 2.3, 6; 1 Jn 4.8, 12, 16), and sacrificing their lives as his friends (15.13-14). They indeed know the truth and live accordingly (1 Jn 2.14; 3.1; 4.5-8; 2 Jn 1-3; 3 Jn 3).

Obviously, such an intimate relationship presupposes *communication*. In God's family, communication *inter alia* takes place in the form of prayer, based on the open relationship within which believers have confidence to approach their Father. Because *Jesus* is sure that the Father always hears his prayers (11.41-42; 11.22), he communicates freely with his Father (11.41-42; 14.16; 16.26; 17.1-26). Like Jesus the *disciples* should also pray with confidence (14.13-14; 15.7, 16; 16.23-26; 1 Jn 3.21-22; 5.14) in the name of, and in obedience to Jesus

(14.13, 14; 15.16; 16.23-27; 1 Jn 3.22). Through prayer believers may ask for whatever they need in order to fulfil their duty and remain true to the wishes of their Father (15.16-17; 1 Jn 5.14-15). This implies that the will of the believer should be synchronized with that of the Son and the Father (5.14) to such an extent that whatever the believer asks, will be granted because it is an expression of the will of the Father.

On the other hand, unbelievers are described as simply having no relationship whatsoever with the Father and Son. That is their basic problem, causing them to be spiritually dead (5.24). They cannot relate to or understand believers at all (1 Jn 3.6; 4.6-8) and do not recognize the Spirit of truth (14.16-17).

6.2.2 The expected behaviour in the family (ethics)

In analogy with ordinary children in an earthly family, the children of God are expected to behave according to the requirements of their families – they should behave as children of God.

A basic ethical assumption is that children should obey their fathers. Children of ancient families were expected to behave according to the tradition of their family as expressed in the wishes of their father. The father was the head of the family who knew the traditions and character of the family. His task was to safeguard those traditions and make sure his children would learn and protect those family traditions. Children were therefore obliged to follow the will of the Father in obedience if they wanted to stay part of that family; as Jesus says, '(children) *do* what you have *heard* from your Father' (8.38; see also 8.41). That is why education was so important. Children had to learn what was expected of them (8.31). This was the responsibility of the father but he could delegate it to someone whom he trusted.

No wonder one of Jesus' titles is 'teacher' (1.38, 11.28; 13.13-14). Jesus instructed the believers by setting them a clear example and giving them ethical commands (13.15; 34-35). Whoever obeys Jesus' commands will illustrate that he or she belongs to the family of God and will be loved by the Father (14.15, 23-24; 15.10, 16-17). This instruction is be continued by the Spirit-*Paraclete*. He will guide and teach believers and remind them of everything that Jesus said (14.26; 16.13-15). Being educated in this way, believers know how to behave and what to do. Children of God will indeed do the will of their Father.

Jesus reveals and mediates the will of the Father to his family. Jesus' food is to do the will of the Father (4.34). If others want to know what the works of God are, they should follow his guidance (6.28-29), as it is stated in 1 Jn 2.6: 'he who says he abides in him (Jesus) ought to walk in the same way in which he walked'. As a branch stays in a vine, believers should stay in Jesus, or else they will not be able to do anything (15.5). Thus it was not a set of rules, but the attitude and behaviour of Jesus, actualized in believers through the Spirit (14.15-19; 15.26-27; 16.5-16; 1 Jn 2.20, 27; 3.24), that serve as an ethical guideline. Jesus actually left his disciples with a concrete example of what is expected of them: he, as their Lord, washed their feet as a supreme token of love and service (13.1ff., 15). They should do likewise.

The heart of Christian behaviour is love for one another. The essence of Jesus' loving example of the footwashing is expressed in the following words: 'A new commandment I give to you, that you love one another; as I have loved you, that you also love one another' (13.34-35). Behaviour in the family of God should be determined by love, since love goes back to God himself (1 Jn 4.10-11, 16-17) and is revealed to us through Jesus. But first, we should establish what exactly love is according to the Gospel in order to avoid misunderstanding.

Jesus is our primary example of love. As the One who makes the Father known, he illustrates what love is. He gave his disciples the example of self-sacrificing love, not only by washing their feet, but also by dying on their behalf (10.11ff.; 12.23-26; 15.12-14; 1 Jn 3.16). They should follow his example and continue his mission (13.15; 17.18; 20.21-23). As their Lord and Teacher did, they should also do – they should love as Jesus loved them (13.34-35; 15.9-12). In the Letters this aspect is emphasized much more strongly. Believers should be righteous and pure like Jesus (1 Jn 3.3, 7), they ought to behave like him (1 Jn 1.7; 2.6) even to the point of laying down their lives like him (1 Jn 3.16). His life and attitude should form the pattern for the lives of his followers. As branches stay in a vine, believers should stay in Jesus. Without him, they can do nothing – strong words indeed (15.4-5). Imitating Jesus is the essence of ethical behaviour in the Gospel.

Love clearly becomes apparent in *actions driven by loyalty and responsibility towards others.* Love is always expressed in terms of *actions* as Jesus himself illustrated by laying down his life for his sheep (10.11-18). It is never just a pure emotion. When God loves, he gives his Son (3.16); when Jesus loves, he gives his life so that people may have life (10.11ff.); when the disciples love, they help others (1 Jn 3.16-18). A few things need to be said about the nature of love.

Love is driven by *loyalty* and *responsibility*, rather than by emotion. Believers must not help others because they 'feel' so much for them, but because Jesus expects it from them. In loyalty to God and in the responsibility towards him because he loved them first (1 Jn 4.10, 19), they should respond in love to others (1 Jn 4.11). Even if you do not like somebody, loyalty and responsibility will force you to act according to the needs of that person.

God's love is indeed a family love – everybody in the family should love everybody else. Love is described in terms of total *reciprocity* – the Father should love the Son and vice versa (15.9-10), the Father should love believers and vice versa (1 Jn 4.16, 20; 5.2-3), the Son should love believers and vice versa (13.34; 14.15, 23), and believers should love one another (13.34-35). Whoever loves God should also love his brother or sister (1 Jn 4.21; 5.1). In this way a network of loyalty and responsibility is woven across the family as part of its social fibre. If somebody is in need he or she should therefore be helped (1 Jn 3.17). No matter what the situation; believers should act in favour of the benefit of their family members (1 Jn 2.10; 3.10, 11, 14, 23; 4.7, 11, 12, 21; 5.1-3), since in this way their love for the Father is also expressed (1 Jn 2.15; 4.19-21; 5.1-3). By describing love in this way, *all* possible situations are covered, because the simple question that determines what the loving action in a particular situation should be is: how can I be of benefit to my brother? Love is thus constantly focused on keeping, protecting and helping family members. Ethical conduct is therefore not a starting point, but a result of being born into the family of God with all the implications associated with that.

Obedience is intricately linked to love. It is the loving response of a person for love received. That is why believers also respond in obedience by doing the will of the Father and the Son (15.12-17; 1 Jn 5.1-3). They are willing to obediently serve the family by washing feet (chapter 13), giving to others what is needed (1 Jn 3.17) and continuing the loving mission of the Father (17.18; 20.21-22). Their behaviour should be visible, since the world should be able to identify the believers through their love for one another (13.34-35). Like Jesus' love for his Father, their love should become visible through their obedience and witness. They should be inspired by Jesus' willingness to die for other members of the family (10.11-18; 15.9-10; 1 Jn 3.17). Their 'death' might not be 'real physical death' but only self-denial, although they should also be willing to lose their lives in service of the Lord (12.24-26; 16.2; 21.18-19). Hating their own lives means being willing to serve as their Lord served; to be where he is and to do what he did (12.25-26; 1 Jn 3.16-17).

But what about *unbelievers*? A criticism levelled at the Johannine documents is that they only focus on 'brotherly love' and it is true that the Gospel primarily focuses on love for fellow believers – they should love one another (13.34; 1 Jn 2.15; 3.17; 4.9, 11, 16). Does this mean that they should not love non-believers? Here the analogy with earthly families helps us to understand what John wants to say. We have seen that children should act like their fathers, also the children of God. God, the Father of the believers, so loved the world that he gave his Son to save them (3.16). Like their Father, believers should also love the world; however, this love should have a soteriological agenda, like the love of their Father. Their love should aim at helping non-believers to become part of the family of God.

But what if a believer does not love as he or she is supposed to? Is there forgiveness for sins?

The Gospel emphasizes that the one sin a person should not commit is rejecting Jesus. Little attention is given to individual wrongdoings in the Gospel, since these are only symptoms of the deadly sin, not accepting Jesus. Consequently, we do not read much about expiation or forgiveness of individual sins in the Gospel. The Letters are different though, since one of the problems addressed there is that of believers sinning by making mistakes and doing the wrong things. How should these 'sinful deeds' be handled? The Letters give us the answer.

Three different types of *sin* are distinguished in 1 John:

- sin as wrongful deeds that are part of the life of every believer (1 Jn 1.8, 10);
- apparently contrasting this view is the statement that a child of God *cannot* sin (1 Jn 3.9-10);
- in 1 Jn 5.16-17 we find a distinction between sin that is to death and sin that is not to death. Let us briefly investigate each of these.

(a) A child of God can and indeed does sin (1 Jn 1.8, 10). Nobody is perfect. We all do wrong things. If we claim that we do not sin (do things against God's will) we lie and actually sin by maintaining that. Transgressions of the will of the father of course do not make the existing relation between a father and a child invalid, but they do create some tension. It becomes necessary for the relationship to be restored to normal. Within family life, there are mechanisms for doing that. This is what the confession of sins is all about (1 Jn 1.8–2.2). The blood of Jesus cleanses people from sin (1 Jn 1.7) and thus the relationship between the believer and God is restored (1 Jn 1.9). Confession in the 'atmosphere' of the expiatory work of Jesus can restore the strained relationship. The presence of Jesus, the 'advocate/special helper' (Gr. = *paraklētos*) who is the propitiation for our sin (1 Jn 2.2; 4.10) with the Father makes all the difference. Jesus as the propitiation for our sins (1 Jn 2.2; 4.10) might refer to the

'payment/punishment' which was required for correcting the wrong being done. In this case it is provided by the 'Special Helper', Jesus, on behalf of the trespasser.

The problems in 2 and 3 John should be seen within this perspective. The bad behaviour of Diotrephes will be addressed, and the relations (also the relations of authority) will be corrected (3 Jn 9-10). In 2 Jn 10-11 the believer should shield himself against being drawn into a situation where evil deeds become a possibility.

(b) The remark in 1 Jn 3.9 that a child of God *cannot sin* is of course notoriously difficult in the light of what was just said, namely, that a child of God does indeed sin. However, the word 'sin' is used with a different meaning in 1 Jn 3.9 than in 1 Jn 1.8-10.

The solution to the problem lies in the phrase in 1 Jn 3.9 referring to 'being born from God'. Good children should strive to do what their father requires and indeed they did. They did not wish to do anything else and did not even harbour any such thoughts, since being part of that family means sharing the identity and traditions of that family, and most definitely not harming the family or disgracing them. This obligation echoes through the whole letter (1 Jn 1.6; 2.3-4, 5, 29; 3.6, 11, 22, 24; 4.20-21; 5.3, 18). It was not something voluntary, and not obliging was seen as acting against one's 'social nature' and was viewed in a negative way.

This forms the social framework for understanding the phrase 'cannot sin' in 1 Jn 3.9. 'Cannot' should therefore be interpreted as 'will not', or 'does not want to, or think of' doing contrary to the will of the heavenly Father. Children of the devil follow their traditions (1 Jn 3.10) and children of God theirs. Doing wrong things (sinning in the sense of 1 Jn 1.8-10) should never become a pattern in the lives of believers. If you make a mistake, you have the option of confessing your sins (1 Jn 1.8–2.2).

(c) The reference to *mortal sin* in 1 Jn 5.16-17 is also notoriously difficult, especially in light of the remark that one should not even pray for such a person. Within the broader theological perspective of the Letter and the Gospel, this seems to refer to unbelief, that is the deliberate choice of not accepting Jesus. In the Gospel those who do not believe will die in their sins (8.24). There is no way in which they will be able to find God. There is no alternative for them. It might even be that the focus is on those who left the community and are now identified as the antichrists (1 Jn 2.18ff.; 2 Jn 7). From a socio-practical point of view there seems to be no reason for them to return to the Johannine group they just left. Hence one should not even pray for them.

6.2.3 Care in the family

As was already pointed out, the family of God is described in analogy to an ordinary earthly family. As you are born into an ordinary family, you are born into God's family; as a child should obey his father in an ordinary family, the children of God should obey God, the Father. As an earthly father was responsible for the care of his family by providing food and protection, God, the Father, had to care for his family by providing *food* and *protection*.

A family is sustained through food and drink. This also applies to the spiritual family of God. Obviously, the food must be of spiritual nature too – that is why Jesus gives spiritual bread and water.

Jesus is the *bread* of life (6.35) that replaces the manna as symbol of God's care (6.31, 49-50). He who 'eats' this bread 'will never hunger or thirst again' (6.35). Jesus himself explains what this means – the person who comes to Jesus in faith will not have spiritual hunger or thirst any longer. He will live for ever (6.35, 40, 47-48, 50, 58).

The same applies to quenching thirst. Jesus offers the Samaritan woman living water. Whoever drinks this water will never thirst again, but 'the water that I shall give him will become in him a spring of water welling up to eternal life' (4.10, 14; see also 7.38-39). He who believes in Jesus will never experience spiritual thirst again (6.35).

Excursus: *Sacraments?* John never mentions the Eucharist. Jesus' last supper with his disciples also shows no sign of the Eucharistic tradition – Jesus washes the feet of his disciples instead of inaugurating the Eucharist (ch. 13). Nevertheless, in 6.51c-59 we have the command to eat Jesus' flesh and drink his blood – clearly sacramental (Eucharistic) language. If John was pro-Eucharist why did he not mention it? If he was anti-Eucharist, why did he include 6.51ff.? The same applies to baptism. Jesus does not ask his disciples to baptize others when he gives them final commands in the last chapters of the Gospel, although his disciples did baptize according to 4.2, and there might be allusions to baptism in verses like 3.5 or 19.34, though incidental. What was John's attitude towards sacraments?

Opinions vary from John not being interested in sacraments (anti-sacramentarian), to a later redactor adding references to sacraments to escape criticism from other Christian groups, to John deliberately changing established views on sacraments because they were over-emphasized, to the understanding that he was a sacramentalist – he took sacraments for granted and saw no need to mention them explicitly. Each of these views tries to argue from the textual material mentioned above. Some argue that the spiritual side of the sacraments is emphasized in the Gospel, others argue that in line with ancient practices of vilification, John wanted to do the opposite – he used Eucharist language in 6.51c but does not directly refer to any ritual practice by name in order to downgrade the activity as such. He wanted to shift the emphasis from the actual cultic activity to the meaning and significance of the sacrament itself. It is not the ritual but Jesus that makes the difference. This debate is still unresolved. Most scholars would accept that there are sacramental overtones in the Gospel, but differ on the reasons why these overtones are not developed in more detail.

Protection of the family was another of the main responsibilities of a father in the ancient world. Likewise, God's family enjoys his protection. The *Father* not only protects Jesus but also his other children. Jesus knows that he will not be left alone. His Father will always be with him (8.28-29; 16.32), as he will be with all his children (17.12, 15). The believers have a task to fulfil in this world (17.18) and need the support and protection of their Father, and they will get it. Nobody would be able to snatch them out of the Father's hand (10.29).

The children of God are indeed born into the family of God where they are accepted, protected, educated, fed, and helped by the Father of the family. As children they should obediently live according to the will of their Father, doing what he wishes and completing his mission in this world. Living in the family of God defines who and what a believer is and should be. Schematically it may be mapped as in Diagram 2.3:

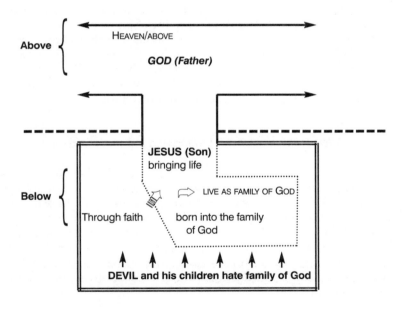

Diagram 2.3

7. The church and the road ahead ... the Spirit, the mission and the future

7.1 Jesus goes back to his Father

After completing his task in this world (17.1-3; 19.30) Jesus, the Lord and Teacher of the disciples, returned to the 'above', that is, to the house of his Father, to prepare room for his followers (14.1-2). This was a dramatic event that would change the history of the Johannine group (chs 14–16). They would be leaderless and without direct guidance when their Lord and Teacher left. However, Jesus tells them not to be sad or discouraged (14.18, 27), since he will not leave them as orphans. He will still take care of them.

Jesus' ascension to heaven is not narrated (both chapters 20 and 21 end with Jesus talking to his disciples), but is well described in the Gospel. Throughout the Gospel Jesus explains that he is from above and must return to the above (8.21-23), to the house of his Father (14.1-2) who sent him (16.5). It is to the advantage of his disciples that he goes away, since the Holy Spirit will come to be with them forever (16.7). For a while, the world will not see him but he will return (14.18-19; 16.16-19). References to Jesus' ascension are mainly part of the imagery of his mission. As any good agent, he came and will return.

7.2 His followers remain behind and are under pressure

The fact is: Jesus' followers were left behind when Jesus left. Fortunately, this would only be for an interim period, since Jesus will return to take them to himself in the Father's house (14.3), where he is (17.24). This promise will be fulfilled on the last day when he raises them up (6.39, 44). The believers would have to survive between the departure and this final return of Jesus. During this period they will have to continue the mission of God in this hostile world among the same people who crucified Jesus. It would be not be an easy road. What awaited them?

(a) *Externally* they were threatened. As followers of Jesus they were seen as dissidents from the true tradition of the followers of Moses and were therefore excluded from the synagogues. Like their Lord they were to be hated, have tribulation, and risk being killed (9.24-34; 15.18ff.; 12.42, 16.2, 33; 17.14). Persecution awaited them and they had to cope with this.

(b) *Internally* there was also reason for their hearts to be troubled and for fear to overtake them (14.27; 16.20, 32). Inner conflict caused serious schisms, leaving the congregation weakened and on the defensive (1 Jn 2.18ff.; 2 Jn 7-11). In 3 John we even see some conflict about authority within the church, and in the Gospel we have evidence of a group under threat where some of Jesus' followers leave him to return to their homes (6.66).

In spite of these trials and dangers, Jesus assured his followers of victory. They will indeed have peace, not the peace of this world, but the peace that Jesus gives (14.27). He has overcome the world (16.33) by judging the prince and ruler of this world (12.31; 14.30). Jesus' victory is also the victory of his followers, as is explained in the Letters. Through their faith in Jesus they overcome this world (1 Jn 4.4; 5.4-5); they are protected by God so that the evil one cannot touch them (1 Jn 5.18; 17.12).

We also sense this delicate balance of the church's existence in this world in Jesus' prayer in chapter 17. In spite of the evil in this world (17.14-16), Jesus does not pray that his followers should be taken out of this world (17.15). He rather prays for their protection as his special sanctified people (17.12-15, 17-19).

There is therefore something paradoxical in being a follower of Jesus. In spite of persecution and tribulation, they have peace, are protected, and are victorious. How is it possible? How should they structure their lives?

7.3 Followers with a mission

God expects his children in this world to be what they are: members of God's family. They are part of God's group of people in this world and this group should be the determining fact in their identity. They should obediently serve the interests of the family by following the example of the unique Son. Their major task would be to continue the mission of God that was started by the Son. That is why, as he left, Jesus *sent* his disciples as the Father had sent him (20.21; 17.18). The disciples are sent into a world that hates and persecutes them (15.18ff.), but they are sent with a life-giving and victorious message – a message of the grace and love of God that offers eternal life to everybody. They had to imitate and represent Jesus in this world by following his example and testifying about him (15.27).

As Jesus imitates the Father by saying and doing what the Father has shown and told him, the disciples must be his imitators. They must be one as the Father and Son are one (17.11, 21-23). As branches stay in the vine, they should stay in Jesus (15.1-8). What Jesus taught and showed them, his words and love (13.34; 15.7-12), should stay in them and regulate their lives. As 1 Jn 2.6 says, 'whoever says, "I abide in him", ought to walk just as he walked' (1 Jn 3.3, 7, 16; 4.17). Believers should be for this world what Jesus had been when he was in this world.

Yes, Jesus was the life to this world, now the believers are the carriers of life in the world (3.16; 1 Jn 5.12) who can offer life to the world. As Jesus was the light of the world (8.12) believers are now children (sons) of *light* (3.21; 12.36); as Jesus was the truth (14.6) believers now know the *truth* and are of the truth (1 Jn 3.19; 2 Jn 1, 4; 3 Jn 3-4). If one now asks where these divine qualities of life or light or truth are to be found in this world, the answer is: wherever the followers of Jesus are. The family of God lives in this world and now reveals and represents the divine reality with all its qualities in this world. In this way they can continue the mission of Jesus. They should be for this world what he was.

But there is also an internal dimension to the mission. As Jesus gathered his people and cared for them, believers should also care for one another in the same way. They should glorify God by being Jesus' friend as well as one another's friends even to the point of death (15.13-17). In 1 Jn 3.16-18 this 'death' like Jesus is symbolically described in terms of caring and helping fellow believers in their time of need. They should follow Jesus' example of love and service by washing one another's feet (13.15). Serving Jesus means total obedience, total commitment, total love that is best expressed in the behaviour of the believer towards others.

Obviously one can ask whether the believers are up to this challenge? Can they really continue the mission of Jesus in this world without the physical presence of their Lord and Teacher, Jesus? Jesus took care of that also.

7.4 The presence of the 'absent' Jesus

Although Jesus went back to his Father, he nevertheless declared: 'I will not leave you orphaned; I am coming to you [after his crucifixion] ... you will see me; because I live, you also will live' (14.18, 23, 28). Somehow the believers will experience the presence of Jesus among them, even after he went back to his Father. He will not be with them in a physical sense any longer, but they will experience his presence in several other ways (14.19-21).

How will believers experience his presence? The key to understanding the presence of Jesus is given in 14.8-14 where it is explained how the Father could be present with the disciples through Jesus. The *modus* of his presence is not physical, but *cognitive* and *functional*. Jesus explains that the Father is present among his disciples through the words and deeds of Jesus. When Jesus speaks and works, it is actually the words and deeds of the Father that they hear and see – the Father works through him (14.10). By listening to Jesus and seeing his deeds, believers hear and see the Father. He is not physically present, but one can experience his active presence and can hear his words.

In the same way Jesus is present in this world through the deeds and words of his followers. Where they act and preach, the works of Jesus are seen and his words are heard. Let's investigate how this is expressed in chapters 14–15.

(a) In 14.12 Jesus says that the believers will do the *work* Jesus did. They will keep his commandments and abide in his love (15.9-10). Like a branch staying in the vine they will stay in Jesus and bear fruit (15.1-8, 16-17). By doing what Jesus asks of them, expressing his love towards others, the presence of Jesus is experienced among these people. Through love Jesus is experienced among them … which makes him functionally present among them.

(b) The expression that the *'words of Jesus* abide' in somebody is equivalent to Jesus abiding in somebody (15.7; 14.23). The expression 'words abide in' was used in ancient times as an indication of a person accepting the teachings and philosophy of a particular school or person. The 'words abiding in him' will determine that person's life – what he says and does. Having the words of Jesus in you means that Jesus determines your thoughts and eventually your deeds. Whenever and wherever you talk or act he becomes visible, since what happens is according to 'his word'. In this way Jesus is cognitively present with his disciples and becomes functionally present through their deeds.

(c) Jesus and the Father are also functionally present through *prayer*. Believers can ask whatever they want *in the name* of Jesus and it will be done by Jesus (14.13). Of course prayer in John is always linked to the will or commandments of Jesus (14.14; 16.24, 26; 1 Jn 5.14-15). This places it squarely in the context of the work and mission of God. Believers may ask Jesus to assist them in fulfilling this mission according to the will of God. And they will experience the helping presence of Jesus among them.

(d) Believers will experience *peace*, not the peace of this world (14.27), but the peace Jesus gives. They will be persecuted 'on account of the name of Jesus' (15.21), because he is their Lord and they therefore represent him, in other words, people 'see' Jesus in them. By persecuting them, they actually also 'persecute' Jesus (15.18-25).

The presence of Jesus is therefore not physical (in that sense he is the *'absent'* one), but cognitive and functional: he is with his followers through his words, deeds, his love, his help when asked, his peace in times of persecution.

But there is another way in which God is present among his children.

7.5 Believers receive a Helper, the Paraclete

7.5.1 The Spirit as *Paraclete*

Meeting his disciples after his resurrection, Jesus sends them into the world to continue his mission. He specially equips them by giving them the Spirit (20.22). Through the power of this Spirit they would be able to continue their missionary task.

A unique characteristic of Johannine literature is that a specific Greek word, *paraclete,* is used to functionally identify the Spirit in the Farewell Discourse(s). The *Paraclete* is identified as the 'Holy Spirit' (14.26) or 'Spirit of truth' (14.16-17; 15.26; 16.13). This is a specific title, used to highlight specific functions of the Spirit. The Spirit also does other things apart from the activities covered by the term *paraclete.* The Spirit is *Paraclete* but the Spirit also does more than a normal *paraclete.* The Spirit gives life (6.63), and also descended and remained on Jesus (1.33) – things that are not normally linked to the work and function of a *paraclete.* (The only other place this term is found in the New Testament is in 1 Jn 2.2 where this title refers to a specific function of Jesus.)

Jesus' departure to his Father is the specific context within which the Spirit is called *Paraclete.* His disciples are staying behind in a hostile world, with a mission … and they will receive special help in the person of the *Paraclete* to assist them. It is insinuated in 14.15-19 that the *Paraclete* could even be linked to the return of Jesus himself, but from the rest of the context it remains clear that Jesus never becomes the *Paraclete.*

The difficulty in pinning down the function of the *Paraclete* becomes apparent when one compares different translations of the Bible. The word is, for instance, translated as Helper (ESV, GNT, ISV), Comforter

(KJV, ASV), Advocate (NAB, NRSV), Counsellor (NIV, NLT), Helper (TEV), and so on. There is not enough evidence from extra-biblical material to conclude that one specific translation is more correct than the others. One is therefore dependent on the functional use of the word in this context to determine what is intended and then come to a proper translation. As will become apparent, the *Paraclete* has a variety of functions all related to assisting believers to survive in a hostile world. That is perhaps the major reason why a single word cannot be found to cover the spectrum of what the *Paraclete* does – he does many things.

7.5.2 The *Paraclete* as special Helper
Based on the intimate relationship between the Spirit-*Paraclete* and the believers (14.16-17), the *Paraclete* performs *specific tasks* among the believers.

(1) The *Paraclete* is intimately involved with the *believers* (internally).

(a)   The *Paraclete* is the *tutor* and mentor of the community, based on the revelation and words of Jesus. He 'will teach you all things and bring to your remembrance all that I have said to you' (14.26). The *Paraclete* brings *Jesus strongly into focus* and thus glorifies him (16.14). This function of the Spirit is confirmed in 1 Jn 2.27. Through the Spirit the education of believers continues. The *Paraclete* or 'anointing' (1 Jn 2.27) was responsible for educating and guiding the community according to the teaching of Jesus that he received and heard from the Father (5.19ff.). A brief note: instead of being called the *Paraclete* in the Letters, the word 'the anointing' (Gr. = *chrisma*) is used to indicate his function of guiding and guaranteeing the truth among believers (1 Jn 2.26-27). 'Anointing' is a strange name for the Spirit, but it again focuses on the function of the Spirit in a specific situation where the teachings of the community were under pressure from the opponents, the so-called 'antichrists' (1 Jn 2.18ff.). In the conflict with the 'antichrists' they do not need anybody to teach them, since 'the Anointing' teaches them everything, and the Anointing 'is true and cannot lie'. The Spirit ('Anointing') serves as guarantee that they are in the truth. They should just make sure that they abide in the Spirit (1 Jn 2.27).

(b)   The *Paraclete guides* the community in truth through the challenges that lie ahead of them, even if it means revealing to them more than Jesus revealed to the original disciples (16.12-13). These new words will rest on the authority of the Father and Son in any case (16.12-14). There is no reason for believers to be unsure of what is expected of them and what they should do (1 Jn 2.26-28). The *Paraclete* will guide them.

(c)   The *Paraclete* also guarantees an *intimate relationship* between the Father, Jesus and the believers. Jesus and his disciples are inseparably linked, even after his resurrection (15.1-8). The *Paraclete* is a key in maintaining this intimate relation (14.16-20), since he will be *in* the believers (14.17). The *Paraclete* indeed ensures the presence of God in believers, which distinguishes them from the world (1 Jn 4.4-6).

(2) The *Paraclete* also helps the believers externally in this *world*.
Witnessing to Jesus is one of the major functions of the *Paraclete*, obviously through the believers (15.26-27). In 16.7-11 there is a strong focus on specific things the *Paraclete* does in relation to this world. He will convict the world concerning sin and righteousness and judgement' (16.7-8). This conviction has strong forensic undertones since it is the task of a judge or advocate to expose wrongdoings and convict them. The *Paraclete* creates the 'atmosphere of the last judgement days' on earth by clearly distinguishing between those who sin by not believing in Jesus and those who indeed believe (16.7-11).

These *Paraclete*-passages in the Gospel are the clearest examples of personification of the Holy Spirit in the New Testament. As *Paraclete* he acts like a person. This brings some to believe that the *Paraclete* is the alter-ego of Jesus. Others are of the opinion that the *Paraclete* should functionally be equated to the leader of the Johannine group, perhaps the Beloved Disciple, since the *Paraclete* leads the believers in truth and teaches them, as did the Beloved Disciple (19.35, 21.24). What the Beloved Disciple witnessed about Jesus was the inspired work of the *Paraclete* in the community. Efforts to identify the exact identity of the *Paraclete* will continue, however the function of the *Paraclete* among the believers is clear.

7.6 The Holy Spirit

Apart from what the Holy Spirit does under the title *Paraclete* in the Farewell Discourse(s) or as the *Anointing* in 1 John, the Spirit is also active on other levels.

(a)   Much of what happens in the Gospel happens through the power of the Spirit. Jesus received the Spirit without measure from his

Father (3.34). As John the Baptist declares (1.32-33), he again baptized the disciples with the Spirit to continue his mission (20.22; 7.38-39). The Spirit is indeed present and active in what Jesus and his disciple do.

(b) The Spirit is the soteriological agent, giving eternal life (6.63) through birth from above (3.3, 5).

(c) In line with what the *Paraclete* does, the Spirit also facilitates the relationship with the Father, but goes even further. True worship of the Father will take place in the Spirit (4.23, 24). The presence of the Spirit is therefore the proof of the intimate relation between the believers and their Father (1 Jn 3.24; 4.13).

(d) The Spirit is often linked to the truth in the Johannine writings. He is called the 'Spirit of truth' (14.17; 15.26; 1 Jn 5.6) who will lead them in truth (16.13). The true Spirit could therefore be distinguished from false spirits by the truth of his witness about Jesus (1 Jn 4.1-3). People who do not listen to this message or to the community show themselves to be in error and as having the spirit of error (1 Jn 4.6).

The Spirit forms the important link between the Father and the believers, cultivating that relationship, equipping believers for that relationship, not only by giving them birth and life, but also by guiding them in truth and protecting them against error. The Spirit also continues the mission of Jesus by remaining with the believers. The Spirit is indeed God's active presence among his children in this world. See Diagram 2.4.

7.7 The eschatological future

According to John those who believe receive eternal life and will not come into judgement. They do not have to wait to inherit life at the last judgement day like the rich young man (Mk 10.17-31, *par.*) or receive it as an eschatological reward on the last day, as Paul says in Romans 6.22-23. In John eternal life seems to be realized here and now while in the synoptics and Paul it still lies in the future. This difference resulted in considerable debates about the relationship between the realized eschatology of John and the futuristic eschatology of other books in the New Testament.

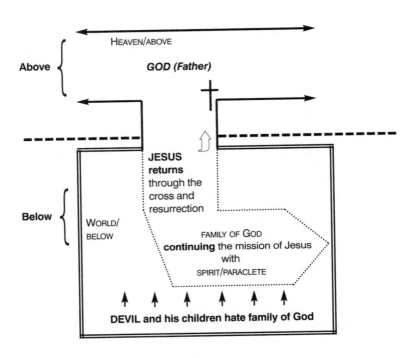

Diagram 2.4

7.7.1 Not a realized or futuristic eschatology, but a progressively realizing eschatology

The eschatological evidence in the Gospel is mixed. In 5.24-29 references to realized and futuristic eschatology appear in the same close context. According to the Gospel believers have eternal life now and will not be judged (they are already God's children). On the other hand there are clear indications of a future eschatology (things are still to happen in the future) in the Gospel too (e.g. 6.39; 14.1-2; 17.24). In 6.54 there is a reference to the present and future eschatology in the same verse (see also 6.39, 40, 44, 47, 51, 54, 58). In the Letters of John the futuristic eschatology is expressed in even clearer terms: 'what we will be has not yet been revealed. What we do know is this: when he is revealed, we will be like him, for we will see him as he is' (1 John 3.2).

Is there a proper explanation for this tension between realized and futuristic eschatology in the Johannine literature? Some argue that all references to future eschatology were not part of the original Gospel, but were added by later redactors, but such a radical suggestion does not really seem necessary. We have seen that eternal life is a state of being, or existence, which makes participation in the spiritual family of God possible. In this family of God the believer has not received everything yet, although he or she already has eternal life (just as a child who lives at birth has not received everything life has to offer simply because he or she lives). What was received is the ability to live (exist) in a family and *progressively experience* what the family has to offer (in the same way that a newborn in the family will progressively experience everything that particular family has to offer). All God's children have eternal life and what it has to offer, but this life is still unfolding into the future (when they will go to the house Jesus prepared and will be where he is – 14.1-3; 17.24, after they are raised up on the last day – 6.39, 54).

This is a situation in which life is constantly realizing itself – it is being lived. As the person having life moves into new situations he or she must 'live' in those situations and thus realize their eschatological existence as members of the family of God. Believers have eternal life now, but they are not taken out of this world yet. Thus they must realize their new eschatological existence right here. They will continuously experience the gifts of the Father, like his protection, his love, his guidance, in this life, while some gifts still await them. In the future there will be a *last day* when the believers who died physically, but have eternal life, will receive their physical bodies back (6.39, 44, 54).

Eternal life implies not that a person has eschatological fullness yet (and it is therefore misleading only to speak of a realized eschatology in John), but that a person has the ability to be part of the spiritual family of God and as such experience whatever the future may offer. In this sense one can speak of a *progressively realizing situation*, being part of the family of God. The members of the family are on their way to the house of the Father (14.1-2), but are still left in this world where they are endangered and need protection (17.15). They must still continue the mission of Jesus (17.18) and will sometime in the future be with the Son where he is (17.24). However, on their way they will experience hatred and persecution in this world (15.18ff.), antichrists in their midst (1 and 2 John), people not living according to the truth (3 John). Nevertheless, through all this they already experience eternal life. There is no point in the future where they will have more life or another life compared with what they have now. They will, however, increase in their experience of being part of the family of God – they are part of a *progressively realizing eschatology*.

7.7.2 The last day...
Johannine believers therefore also await the 'last day' like other early Christians (6.39-40). What are they to expect?

(a) The day of judgement for unbelievers
In 12.48 the words of Jesus are self-explanatory: 'The one who rejects me and does not receive my word has a judge; on the last day the word that I have spoken will serve as judge.' Believers are not judged, since they already have eternal life (3.16-18). Judgement is already passed on them ... they are God's children (3.18). On the other hand, those who do not believe are already condemned by the words of Jesus that whoever does not believe will endure God's wrath and perish (3.18, 36). On the last day their fate will be sealed (12.48). However, the Judge has spoken now already: those who believe have eternal life, but those who do not believe in him will perish.

(b) Believers will be raised
References to the '*last day*' in the Gospel are restricted to a few remarks in chapter 6. Jesus will raise the believers on the last day, most probably physically (6.39, 44, 54). That they can expect something in the future is also clear from passages with a futuristic eschatological undertone like 14.1-2 where Jesus goes away to prepare room for them in the Father's house, or in 17.24 where Jesus prays that the believers may one day be where he is, with his Father, and experience his glory.

The clearest reference to a futuristic eschatology is in 1 Jn 3.1-2 where it is said that believers already have eternal life, but what they will be is not yet revealed. The eschatological process is still progressively realizing itself. In the future, when Jesus comes and is revealed, they will see Jesus as he is, because they will be like him and be with him. Schematically it may be mapped as in Diagram 2.5.

8. Conclusion

In this theological analysis, we systematized and related the theological content of the Gospel and Letters. The theological structure is based on the salvific mission of Jesus by his Father. Jesus was sent to bring life, light, and freedom to people who were in darkness and were slaves of sin. Anybody who believes in Jesus is born from above, receives eternal life, and becomes part of the family of God. When Jesus returns to his Father, this family must continue his salvific mission in this world through the guidance of the Spirit-*Paraclete*. Believers should

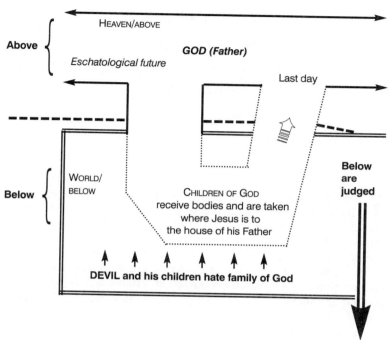

Diagram 2.5

remain in Jesus, by keeping his words and commandments and by believing in him as Jesus, the Son of God. Eventually, Jesus will take them to the glorious house of his Father, where he is now.

This brings us to questions with a more historical flavour. Who wrote this Gospel? Where did the message come from and what influenced the author to write in the manner he did? Why does this Gospel differ so much from the others on literary and theological levels? These and similar questions form part of the larger historical, theological, and scientific investigation of the Gospel material. Being familiar with the content and message of the Gospel and Letters, we can now consider these other questions. We must however remember that the message of these documents cannot be separated or considered in isolation from what follows. Decisions related to the date of composition, socio-cultural influences on the Johannine group, and so on. have an impact on the way one understands the contents and message of the Gospel too. We will take that into account as we consider the other issues.

3

The Gospel and Letters of John in relation to Other Similar Documents

The Johannine Gospel and Letters have a very particular message and a particular manner of expressing that message; this has already been discussed in the previous chapters. Having had an overview of the contents of these documents, we can now ask *where these contents came from*. This question has to do with what is usually called *source criticism*. Knowing the roots of the Johannine documents as well as their relation to other similar documents (like the other Gospels or even the Old Testament) will help a lot in determining the early Christian tradition and its development.

The Gospel and Letters form part of the volume of books that the Christian Church from very early on regarded as their normative basis, their canon (rules). Obviously, if you could ask the early Christians whether they would scatter these books through the whole library of ancient documents or group them together on one shelf because of their close affinity, they would choose the latter. These documents belong together. As such, these documents have special status and authority among Christians and indeed played crucial roles in the formation of Christianity and the formulation of dogma in the Church. Because of their special status as part of the canon they are mostly read and studied as part of and in the light of the other documents in that canon (canonical criticism), except where the interest relates specifically to the historical value of these documents within early (Christian) history (historical criticism).

Excursus: *How did the Gospel and Letters become part of the canon?* The 'canonical histories' of the Gospel and Letters differ, and their inclusion in the Bible was not without some difficulty.

The inclusion of the *Gospel* according to John into the list of authoritative Christian documents largely happened in the second century. Its authority becomes apparent when Tatian (2nd century) uses the chronological frame of the Fourth Gospel for processing the other three in his *Diatesseron*. Others, like Theophilus of Antioch (ca.

180 CE) quoted from the Gospel, and other important church fathers like Clement of Alexandria, Origen, and Tertullian accepted its authority. There were, however, some complicating factors.

(a) One such complicating factor was the favour the Gospel carried with the Gnostics in the second century. Especially Valentinian Gnostics appealed to this Gospel in support of their views of Jesus and the nature of Christian existence. The first commentary on the Gospel was even written by a Gnostic, Heracleon. This caused scepticism about the status of the Gospel within some early Christian circles. However, a church father from the second century, Irenaeus, appealed to the very same Gospel in his book, *Against Heresies* (ca. 180 CE), to argue for the orthodox faith against Gnostic beliefs. This restored the status of the Gospel.

(b) In the Eastern Church there were also some feelings among the anti-Montanists against the Gospel, resulting from their debates with the Montanists. The 'Alogi' were also not so favourable towards the Gospel; they even ascribed the authorship to Cerinthus (a Gnostic teacher from about the turn of the first century). Neither the Montanists or the 'Alogi' had a large following and the authority of the Gospel was soon confirmed – it was included in the earliest list of the 'Muratorian Canon' (generally dated 180–200 CE) and was secured as part of the canon through the ecumenical decisions of the church in the fourth century.

The three *Letters* were at first not treated as a group and were only described as 'Johannine letters' in the late second century. Because 1 John was more closely linked to the Gospel than 2 and 3 John, it received recognition first. At least Irenaeus (approximately 180 CE) was convinced John was the author of 1 John and apparently quoted from this Letter in his *Against Heresies*. The acceptance of 2 and 3 John took longer than 1 John and their brevity caused some problems. Although Eusebius (4th century) regarded 2 and 3 John as well known and recognized by most, he nevertheless placed them among the disputed books. However, it is plausible that 1 and 2 John could have been regarded as authoritative by the middle or latter part of the second century; they seem to be part of the Muratorian Canon (end of second century). At the end of the fourth century all three Letters were acknowledged as canonical, although the Eastern church's final recognition had to wait until the fifth century.

1. The relationship between John and the synoptics

1.1 The problem

From the earliest times, the Gospel of John was grouped with the other three Gospels, Matthew, Mark and Luke. Like the other Gospels John also narrates the life and teachings of Jesus. One would expect narratives about the same person and historical events to be roughly similar in structure and even language. This is the case with the three synoptic Gospels (Matthew, Mark and Luke), but the Gospel of John does not seem to fit their common pattern. The presentation of the person and history of Jesus differs on significant points from the other Gospels.

How should we deal with these different and often conflicting historical presentations of the same events in the life of Jesus? Obviously, one would have to ask which presentation is more accurate … and this opens a beehive of discussion, being stung to active discussion by questions like which one was dependent on the other, which tradition is the oldest and most reliable, what is the historical value of the different Gospels, and so on. This is exactly the beehive one lands in by asking the question about the relationship between John and the synoptics. It became one of the major issues in Johannine research.

1.2 The implications of answers to the problem – a methodological remark

Before we take a closer look at the differences and similarities between the different Gospels, we should ask a methodological question. Why is the issue of the relationship between John and the synoptics so important that it became a major discussion in Johannine research? Does it really matter whether John's Gospel was dependent on the synoptics or not? Should we really spend time on it? It is important to realize that with the answer given to this question many of your cards are already put on the table as to how you are going to interpret the Gospel of John. This issue is related to many other issues in the interpretation of John and has definite implications for the interpretation of the Gospel material. Therefore, we need to consider some of these implications.

If you, for instance, say that John was dependent on the synoptics, it implies that John must have been written *later* than the synoptics. This implies a later *date* of composition and also leaves a shorter time for creative impact by the Johannine group itself on the final text (for those who want to argue that John was composed over a lengthy period of time).

It would also have implications for the *historical reliability* of John. If John was dependent on the synoptics it seems logical to many that the Johannine historical material would then be secondary to the synoptics and could therefore not be taken seriously in issues like the quest for the historical Jesus. On the other hand, if John's Gospel developed independently, it could be argued that on certain levels John might even be historically superior to the synoptics, since John might have had access to independent traditions and material that were not

(d) The cleansing of the temple takes place at the beginning of Jesus' ministry in John (2.13-22) while the same event takes place just before the crucifixion of Jesus in the synoptics.

(e) Jesus gives the Spirit to his disciples during one of his last appearances (20.21-22), something the synoptics do not mention.

(f) In the synoptics Peter is most prominent, but in John's Gospel the Beloved Disciple takes greater prominence.

There are also some major differences between the *discourses* of John and those in the synoptics.

(a) *Stylistically* John develops his material in long discourses, something the synoptic Gospels do not do. He does not really use parables but rather develops elaborate imageries through his whole Gospel based on metaphors and symbols; for instance, the imagery of the believers as family of God, or Jesus as an Agent sent by the Father, Jesus as Good Shepherd, Vine, King, or Temple.

(b) John's *vocabulary* also differs from that of the synoptics. (The only instance of direct similarity is in Matthew 11.27, 'All things have been handed over to me by my Father; and no one knows the Son except the Father, and no one knows the Father except the Son and anyone to whom the Son chooses to reveal him' (*par*. Lk. 10.22).) Instead of the kingdom of God John prefers to talk about having eternal life – something that is only promised as a gift in the future in the synoptics; instead of conversion he explains turning to God in terms of faith and rebirth. John does not mention tax collectors and Sadducees, but he refers to Jews and Pharisees. Dualistic terms like light/darkness, truth/lie, life/death, and so on. are favourite terms to describe the qualitative difference between the family of God and the family of the devil. The Jesus of John's Gospel frequently refers to himself with 'I am-sayings' (I am the good shepherd, I am the bread of life, I am the resurrection and life, and so on), something that is rare in the synoptics.

(c) Jesus' miraculous *deeds* are not called miracles in John's Gospel, like in the synoptics, but signs (*semeia*). His miraculous deeds are theologically determined and their significance lies in pointing to Jesus and thus enriching and strengthening his message.

(d) The picture of the *Johannine Jesus*, who is the Word (*Logos* – 1.1) and has the glory of God, being the unique God who is close to the Father's side (1.18), who takes charge of his own death and resurrection (10.17-18), and so on, differs from the synoptic picture of Jesus.

The results of this brief survey of the differences between John and the synoptics highlight some important issues:

(a)   *Pivotal narratives*, namely Jesus' first sign in Cana (2.1-11) and the most important sign (apart from the resurrection), that is, the raising of Lazarus (ch. 11) are not found in any of the synoptics. The Lazarus events are in John's story, so to speak, as the final reason for Jesus' crucifixion. Apart from this, another crucial event, the washing of the disciples' feet (13.1ff.), which serves as a basic ethical example for his disciples, is also not present in the synoptics. These differences are not insignificant, since the broad overarching narrative of John is carried by these pivotal narratives.

(b)   There do, however, seem to be some significant *historical discrepancies* between the synoptics and John's Gospel. Jesus' ministry overlapped with that of the Baptist (3.25-26). He visited Jerusalem more frequently (2.13; 5.1; 7.10), the date of the last meal does not correspond with that mentioned in the synoptics, his gift of the Spirit took place when he was still with his disciples (20.21-22), and so on. This complicates the question of historicity. Although John was for many ages regarded as historically the less reliable Gospel, there are voices (like R. Brown) who argue that John should not just be dismissed – there are Johannine accounts that are more likely to be historically accurate than the synoptic accounts (such as his relation to the Baptist, the longer period of public ministry, and so on).

(c)   There is also a vast difference in *vocabulary* and even *style* that makes even indirect dependence on the synoptics hard to argue for.

One can carry on by pointing out similarities and differences on an even more detailed level, but the above is enough to illustrate the dilemma: was John dependent on the synoptics, and if so, how? If not, where does John come from and why was it written? One should not make the common mistake of just focusing on the material that is similar if you want to argue for dependence, or the other way round. A balanced solution should be sought. One must get to a proper explanation of how it is possible that John could have so many points of contact with the synoptics, but nevertheless presents us with a Gospel so unique and different from the others. How can one do justice to all of this evidence?

1.5 How should the literary problem of the Gospel according to John be solved?

How could the similarities and differences be explained within a single scenario? The similarities most probably point to some form of relationship, knowledge or contact, but how much and how? Why is the relationship so indirect without any direct quotations? How should one treat the significant differences that most probably suggest independence? How can documents be dependent and independent of each other at the same time?

Theories abound – it is almost a matter of there being as many opinions as there are minds. The different suggestions can be divided into three major groups:

- Some accept the *literary dependence* of John on the synoptics. (On the other hand, there are those who argue that Luke was dependent on John.)
- Other scholars' departing point is that John had *no knowledge* of the synoptics. Thus, John was written *independently* from the synoptics.
- Then there are those who suggest *limited dependence* or *independence* if you like. Somehow John was aware of the synoptics and knew their content, but did not consciously rely on them when writing his Gospel.

The most prominent view in the first quarter of the previous century was dependence of John on the synoptics, especially on Mark (supporters are, for instance, Jülicher, Moffat, Zahn, Streeter). In the period following that, the mood changed after the important book of Gardner-Smith and independence became the preferred way of explaining the relationship between John and the synoptics. The issue of dependence was revived in the last third of the previous century due to the work of the 'Louvain school', who argue for a refined form of dependence (other supporters of this view are, for instance, Perrin, Strecker, Schnelle).

These different positions will be briefly explained. Obviously different authors give different slants to the positions they hold – this cannot be reflected in detail here. A broad overview should however suffice:

(a) *Literary dependence* of John on the synoptics
For a long time literary dependence was accepted, based on the similarities discussed above. Since the remark of Clement of Alexandria (153–217 CE) that John is a 'spiritual Gospel' that aims to give a less

restricted, spiritual explanation to the more factual information of the synoptics, the view of dependence was generally accepted. This consensus lasted until the beginning of the previous century. Several other arguments supported this idea. John had deliberately chosen the Gospel genre, which already existed in the form of the synoptics, which implies that John obviously knew the synoptics and used them. However, it was not a matter of cut and paste, rather John selectively used and thoroughly edited and reworked the synoptic material (Barrett), which simultaneously explains the differences among the similarities. Affinities and similarities are pointed out especially based on the passion narratives, which should then serve as proof that there is literary dependence of John on Mark or Luke. (There are those who favour the one synoptic Gospel while others favour the other. However, it seems as if Mark is regarded as the strongest possibility if one argues for literary dependence, with Luke following. Matthew is less favoured.)

Variations on this view were developed; for instance, based on the assumption that the Gospel of John developed in different stages over a longer period of time, it is argued that the evangelist did not know the synoptics, but the later editors did. It is then argued that John represented an independent tradition that explains the differences. However, at a later stage of this development the editor of John's Gospel added the synoptic material (earlier Thyen) or alternatively, synoptic material influenced the process of development in different ways at different stages of the relatively long period of development (Brown).

It is because of some unresolved (or perhaps unresolvable) issues that many scholars still remain sceptical about the dependence theory.

To suggest that the editor of John's Gospel used the synoptics begs for deeper explanation on several issues; for instance, synoptic material is concentrated in certain areas of John's Gospel. Why did the editor limit the synoptic influence to these sections and why didn't he add synoptic material to other sections of the Gospel where it would have supported his argument equally well? Why did the editor think that the specific synoptic material he used was so important and that other elements of synoptic material were not?

A complicating factor is that the similarities do not offer a systematic or coherent pattern of usage – the pattern of agreements and disagreements is inconsistent. Material from the same gospel is even used in different ways. This makes it virtually impossible to develop a coherent theory concerning the rationale of editorial changes.

Supporters of this theory tend to suggest hypothetical material in the form of oral sources or even literary sources that existed before the current Gospels. Obviously, these literary (and oral) sources do not exist any longer, since they are hypothetical. This makes verification very difficult and leaves arguments based on them rather vague with little possibility of substantiation.

(b) John was written *independently* from the synoptics

At the other end of the spectrum supporters of independence from the synoptics are found. The important work of Gardner-Smith (already in 1938) and Dodd (1963) put an end to the previously highly regarded view that John's Gospel was dependent on the synoptics. They were of the opinion that John wrote *independently* of the synoptics but made use of traditions parallel to, or at least similar to, the synoptics. Dodd argued that by applying form-critical methodological insights it could be proven that John developed independently from the synoptics. The Johannine material was based on the same type of oral traditions accepted for the synoptics.

The more radical view is that the author(s) of John's Gospel had no knowledge of the synoptics at all (not of sources, neither of later redactional layers) and that he wrote his Gospel independently from the others, based on his own independent traditions and sources (J. Becker, J.A.T. Robinson, S.S. Smalley). That would mean that with Mark and Q, John is another major early source of information of Christianity. In order to explain the similarities between John and the synoptics, it is then argued that there must have been a broad stream of common early Christian tradition that was used by John as well as others in the compilation of their works. This would explain the similarities without implying a particular dependence on the synoptics (R. Kysar, J.L. Martyn, O. Cullmann, F.J. Moloney, E. Käsemann, R. Schnackenburg). A favourite way of explaining this 'big stream of common early Christian traditions' is to argue that a significant oral source underlies all the Gospels. Material from this oral tradition was then taken up by John (and likewise by the synoptics), interpreted, and shaped according to the needs of each particular community, creating its own unique Gospel. In this sense all the Gospels are rooted in such a tradition, which explains the similarities.

Again not all the problems are resolved by supporters of this view. Once more, a hypothetical source or 'big stream of common early Christian tradition' must save the day. Obviously, we do not have such a document or source, which means that every interpreter can construct his own form of such a source according to the needs of his argument. A consistent and convincing theory of exactly what such a source could have looked like is still to be offered.

(c) *Limited dependence* of John on the synoptics

There are some variations of scenarios that acknowledge dependence or at least direct knowledge, or awareness, of the synoptics, but also maintain the independence of John's Gospel – for example the 'in between' position (Bailey, Boismard).

It is maintained that before John was finally committed to text (during the pre-Johannine traditional stage) there was contact with written synoptic material. This contact could have been with oral or written traditions behind the synoptics (pre-Gospel synoptic sources) or with the written synoptic Gospels themselves (Borgen). This contact left a lasting impression on the Johannine tradition. The synoptic material in written form, or perhaps in the memory of the author of John's Gospel, was smoothly integrated into the Johannine material, which explains the similarities between John and the synoptics as we have it today.

Here the 'Louvain school' led by Neirynck and Sabbe must be mentioned. They suggest that John's Gospel was dependent on the synoptics as we have it and not on any underlying source. Their argument is based on the following assumptions:

(i)   that John's Gospel must be compared to the synoptics, because of the similarities in structure and content as well as the fact that all four are Gospels;

(ii) John's Gospel was most probably written later in the first century, which makes some form of literary dependence possible;

(iii) one must allow for creativity in presenting the material – this is typical for all the Gospels;

(iv) the Johannine author's style, vocabulary, themes, and so on, must be studied thoroughly to identify the possible use of sources or transformation of these sources. Special care must be taken, since a unique situation or theme might require unique vocabulary.

H. Thyen (2005) approached the similarities in another way. He defends the position that John knew the synoptics but was not dependent on them but rather used their material with less ardent rigour. That is why there are traces of synoptic material, but not in such a form that literal dependence can be proven. John artfully and loosely reshapes the synoptic material to serve his message.

What should we make of all these suggestions? It is clear that there are valid arguments in each direction, because there are both similarities and differences. It does however seem safer to take an intermediary view that John was written independently, but with some form of contact with synoptic material.

However, in evaluating the different positions one should be aware that often selective argumentation plays a role. For instance, supporters of some form of literary dependence will focus on those texts that are similar and build their argument on that. Often little attention is given to the unique material. On the other hand, those who defend independence will emphasize the considerable differences and minimize the similarities. In forming an opinion, one should be as open as possible to all the available evidence from across the broad spectrum of arguments.

2. The Old Testament

John deliberately refers to or even quotes parts of the Old Testament, such as Isaiah 6.10 or 53.1 (12.38-40), which signifies that the Gospel should be read in the light of the 'Scriptures' (5.39).

The exact relation is not clear and no clear pattern can be easily discerned. It is also not always apparent from which Old Testament texts the quotations were taken (the texts in square brackets are approximations of Old Testament texts – see Menken). There are unmistakable indications of quotations, introduced by 'it was written ...' (2.17 [Ps. 69.10]; 6.31 [Ps. 78.24]; 6.45 [Isa. 54.13]; 10.34 [Ps. 82.8]; 12.14 [Zech. 9.9; Isa. 35.4; 40.9]). Then there are fulfilment quotations, introduced by something akin to 'in order that the Scripture/word of the prophet is fulfilled ...' (12.38-40 [Isa. 6.10; 53.1]; 13.18 [Ps. 41.10]; 15.25 [Ps. 35.19]; 19.24 [Ps. 22.19]; 19.36-37 [Exod. 12.10, 46; Ps. 34.21; Zech. 34.12]). Of course there are also allusions to Old Testament texts, like the imagery of the shepherd (10.1-30 [Pss. 23, 95.7; Ezek. 34]), or the vine (15.1-17 [Ps. 80; Ezek. 17, 19; Hos. 10]).

Where did John get his quotations from? In other words, which Old Testament documents did he use? Many of the quotations come from the Greek translation of the Old Testament (the LXX or Septuagint), while others seem to go back to the Hebrew texts, while in other cases it is not clear where they come from. The overall impression is that John wanted to show the relationship between his Gospel and the message of the Old Testament, but simultaneously used the Old Testament information with great freedom in order to present it as an integral part of his overall message. His point is that the message and prophecies of the Old Testament are fulfilled in the life of Jesus. There is therefore direct dependence on the Old Testament, but the material is reinterpreted in the light of the person and presence of Jesus.

3. What about the Letters?

1–3 John form part of the literary genre of Letters in the New Testament. There are doubts whether 1 John is indeed a letter, since it does not have the usual qualities of a letter (greetings, and so on). When we ask about the dependence of the Johannine Letters on other literature, the only real option is that they were dependent on the Gospel of John. This position, of course, is augmented significantly depending on whether one accepts that they were written before or after the Gospel. They are therefore quite unique in their character and literary appearance in the New Testament.

4. Conclusion

The Johannine literature forms part of the canonical documents and is related to the other Gospels and the Old Testament, although there are some differences of opinion on how these relations should be seen. The possibility must obviously be left open that the Johannine literature also relates to material outside of the canon of Scripture, of which Gnostic (Mandaean), Hellenistic (Philo), Rabbinic, or even Platonic material may be mentioned. These relations will receive attention later on.

The above discussion showed that John's Gospel and Letters are not copies or even thoroughly reworked copies of another document, like a synoptic Gospel. The material is uniquely composed and presents the message of Jesus in a novel way, even though sources might have been used in sections of the Gospel. This brings us to the important question of the literary characteristics of the Johannine texts themselves. What are the literary characteristics of these texts that are so different from, for instance, the synoptics? Did the author(s) use sources or was the Gospel a *de novo* composition? Let us now investigate the specific literary characteristics of the Gospel that resulted in such an interesting and challenging, but also different Gospel from the others.

4

The Composition of the Gospel: Multiple Sources or a Seamless Document?

The literary characteristics of the Gospel of John intrigued scholars for especially two reasons. One reason is the strange 'unevenness' of the text itself. There are sudden apparently illogical breaks in the text or inconsistencies that seem to defy the notion of a single author composing the Gospel. The other reason is the abundant use the author(s) made of symbols, metaphors, and stylistic features like misunderstanding or irony. This makes it a very exciting text to read since it constantly challenges any reader. Giving close attention to these literary characteristics is therefore an important part of analysing the Johannine texts.

1. A highway or a rocky road?

Would the reading experience of the Gospel resemble a smooth trip on a highway, or a trip on a rocky road where one must often slow down to pass problems along the way? Many scholars opt for the rocky road scenario. They report that during their trip through the Gospel they came across strange illogical breaks in the story line – the reader is in Galilee at one point, and then suddenly in Jerusalem the next – or they find that in one part of the Gospel one thing is said while a few pages later the opposite is stated. They do not experience the text as a smooth and well-rounded composition. Diagram 4.1 identifies *different types* of textual problems that could hinder a 'smooth trip' through the Gospel. These different types of textual problems as well as ways to explain these problems will now be considered.

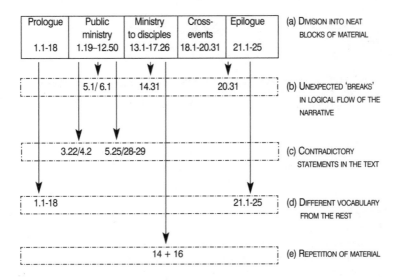

Diagram 4.1

1.1 The material in this Gospel divided into blocks
(a in Diagram 4.1)

The general flow of the narrative seems orderly – Jesus is baptized, and starts out on his public ministry by preaching and performing signs. When things heat up he gathers his disciples around a meal and instructs them about their future. That night he is arrested, is crucified the next day and arises from the grave on the following Sunday, after which he appears to his disciples again.

What immediately catches the eye when reading the Gospel is the *block-like division* of the material. The material is not chronologically but thematically compiled.

(a)   The first twelve chapters cover *three* years of Jesus' *public ministry*. (His message to the world.)

(b)   The next five chapters (13–17) deal with only a *few hours*, i.e., one evening during which Jesus spoke to his *disciples*. (His message to his people.)

(c)   Chapters 18–20 tell us what happened during the next *three days* when Jesus was *crucified* and rose from the grave. (Passion.)

Sign		Discourse	
Water into wine	2.1-11	Explanation of the new life	3.1-21
Healing of the official's son	4.43-54	Jesus is the water of life	4.1-26
Healing at Beth-zatha/Bethesda	5.1-15	Jesus gives life like his Father	5.16-47
Feeding of the five thousand	6.1-15	Jesus is the bread of life	6.22-58
Jesus heals the blind man	9.1-12	The blind man defends Jesus	9.13-34
		Jesus talks to the Jews	9.35-41
		Since he is the light of life	8.12-59
Lazarus is raised from death	11.1-44	Jesus is the resurrection and life, but also the Shepherd	11.25-26
		who lays down his life	10.7-30

This suggests that the author(s) consciously planned the presentation of his (their) material and divided it into neat blocks (see 20.30; 21.25 for conscious selection by the author). Within these 'blocks' another structural feature catches the eye. There are seven (or eight, depending on how one counts) *signs* or miracles in the Gospel. They are all narrated in the first part of the Gospel (1–12), with the exception of the multiplication of the fish in the epilogue (21). What Jesus says (the discourse) is substantiated and illustrated by the accompanying signs. These miracles are usually followed by long discourses, as could be seen from the preceding summary.

The fact that these signs only occur in the first block of material (1–12) and that they may be clearly distinguished from the discourses that seem to have been consciously added, immediately alerts the *source theorists*. They conclude that there must have been some sort of *semeia* (sign) *source* that formed the basis of the first block. Discourses that were later added to the signs could have been taken from a *discourse source*, while the last section in 18–20 was based on a *passion source*. They argue that during the composition of the Gospel different sources could have been added at different stages. Imagine ... at first there was just the story of signs Jesus performed, illustrating how wonderful he was. Soon questions about his person developed and material about the passion narrative had to be added. Now the discussion was really on ... who was he and what did he say? Now was the time to introduce blocks of material on his discourses ... and so on.

On the other hand, scholars argue that it is not necessary to conclude that sources were used, since the theme in the first block, dealing with the gospel to the world, naturally invites signs, while signs were not necessary when Jesus spoke to his disciples alone at the meal. There is therefore a perfectly natural explanation for the signs occurring only in the first block. Elaborate source theories are not necessary. We will return to this discussion in due course.

1.2 A problem: tensions and breaks in the text of the Gospel

In the debate on the use of sources in the Gospel, sudden breaks in the text, contradictions, repetitions, and differences in vocabulary all play an important role in identifying different sets of material or different sources. It is argued that an author would not leave all kinds of contradictions or tensions in the text if he himself composed the text from the beginning. This only happens if one adds material to an already existing text or source. Let us now carefully consider the arguments of those in favour of the idea that the Gospel developed in stages through the combination and integration of different sources.

The 'tensions' in the text will first receive attention, followed by some of the most important theories that were developed to explain these tensions.

(a) Unexpected 'breaks' in the logical flow of the narrative (b in Diagram 4.1)
There are some unexpected and illogical breaks in the flow of the text that suggest 'outside' intervention into the text:

(i)   According to 5.1 the events narrated in chapter 5 take place in *Jerusalem*, that is in Judaea. Suddenly, in chapter 6, Jesus finds himself near the Sea of *Galilee* (6.1). There is no indication how or when he travelled from Jerusalem to Galilee.

(ii) A similar chronological problem occurs in 14.31 where Jesus tells his disciples that they should 'get up and go'. Surprisingly nothing like that happens, since Jesus simply carries on talking for another three chapters (15–17).

(iii) The signs in 2.11 and 4.54 are numbered as one and two. However, in between these two numbered signs other signs are mentioned (2.23). Were these overlooked when the author was initially numbering the signs?

(iv) In 20.30-31 the purpose of the Gospel is formulated and it seems to signify the end of the Gospel. Nevertheless, the narrative continues in chapter 21 with another similar ending. Why do we have two apparent 'endings'?

(b) Contradictions? (c in Diagram 4.1)

Statements like the following raise questions, and need to be explained in a credible way:

(i)   In 3.22 Jesus baptizes, but in 4.2 he does not.

(ii) According to the statement in 5.25 ('the hour is coming, and is now here … and those who hear will live'), it seems as if one already has eternal life, while a repetition in 5.28-29 ('for the hour is coming when all who are in their graves will hear his voice and will come out – those who have done good, to the resurrection of life') seems to imply that eternal life will only be given later.

(iii) According to his brothers Jesus had apparently not done much in Jerusalem. He must return so that his disciples may see what he is capable of (7.3). But, what about his miraculous works at the pool of Bethesda where he healed a cripple (5.2-9), or his other miracles mentioned in 2.23 or 4.45? Surely, his disciples must have seen these?

(iv) In 13.36 Peter asks Jesus where he is going – in 16.5 Jesus claims that nobody asked him that question. The contradiction is apparent.

(c) Differences in vocabulary and repetitions (d and e in Diagram 4.1)

The *vocabulary* used in the Prologue especially, but also in the Epilogue, is markedly different from the vocabulary in the rest of the Gospel. Words used in the Prologue like *Logos* (in its personified usage), grace, or fullness, are not repeated in the rest of the Gospel. The same applies to many words in the Epilogue.

There also seem to be some striking *repetitions*. Compare, for instance, chapters 14 and 16, or the numerous smaller repetitions throughout the Gospel, of which repeated references to life, and the mission of Jesus, are good examples.

Why would any author change his vocabulary on the one hand but also choose to repeat himself so often?

1.3 Suggested solutions for tensions and breaks in the text

What could the solution be to the aforementioned problems in the text? There are basically two different ways that these problems are approached.

A longer period of active involvement by different people (editors/redactors) in shaping the text to its final form is suggested. Some composed the Gospel by using 'blocks' of material (= sources) while others edited it, causing smaller tensions. There are obviously numerous and diverse suggestions as to how this could have happened.

Others suggest that the text is a coherent whole and not a quilt of different sources. The aforementioned tensions could be explained within the confines of the theological or stylistic characteristics of the text itself.

The methodology of these two approaches will now be considered.

1.3.1 A process of development ... sources, redactions, editorial work

For the sake of clarity, theories dealing with major 'blocks' of material (chapters 1–12; 13–17; 18–20) are going to be treated first, followed by theories explaining the tensions in the text, since these suggest two different compositional procedures. However, scholars like Bultmann developed a theory that combines solutions to these different types of problems, mainly by suggesting that initially sources were used while later redactional or editorial work followed, creating the tensions.

Excursus: *How do you identify sources?* 'Sources' are understood as literary, written documents that were available to the original author. There seems to be no single, generally accepted method for *source analysis* of the material in John's Gospel, i.e. distinguishing and analysing different sources used in its composition. However, some of the criteria used are the following:

(a) *Blocks* of different material are distinguished through the use of different *forms* of literature, for instance, miracles (signs), discourses, or the passion narratives. The content and form of a particular text play an important role in identifying something as a miracle, hymn, or discourse. When such a literary form is identified, it is then assumed that it existed in that, or a similar form, before the composition of the current text and that it was as such 'taken over' and added to the current text – something like the use of 'cut and paste' on a computer.

(b) *Literary breaks* or *inconsistencies* in the flow of the text indicate that a text either was added from a source or is evidence of an editor's hand. For Fortna this is foundational in identifying sources – he focuses on breaks, repetitions, tensions and gaps. Once he has identified them, and described the sources on that basis, the next step is to show that these 'sources' differ in style from the rest of the Gospel.

(c) *Stylistic differences* between two texts in the Gospel imply two sources. Bultmann and Fortna see this as one among several criteria that should be used in combination with others to identify sources. On their own, stylistic differences are inconclusive, since the style of the same author may vary.

(d) *'Content criticism'* is used by Bultmann, who maintains that the Evangelist propagated realized eschatology. This automatically caused him to 'brand' all references to future eschatology in the Gospel as later additions.

It is also important to determine the origin of the sources themselves, once they are identified, since that will co-determine the nature and content of the Gospel. However, no fixed methodological procedure exists to guide the process of identifying the original location of the sources that were supposedly used by the author of John.

Although numerous scholars developed diverse source theories, Bultmann and Fortna are the best-known exponents and will serve as examples of the use of source theory in this Gospel. (There will be some repetition of what was already said, since it is important to get a full picture of Bultmann's views.)

Bultmann stands in the exegetical tradition of early twentieth-century literary criticism. In his 1941 commentary, *Evangelium nach Johannes*, he aimed to analyse the prehistory and development of the text of John's Gospel, trying to explain how the present text came into being. His first suggestion was that three sources underly the present text: the 'signs source' (German = *Semeia-Quelle*), a 'revelatory discourse source' (German = *Offenbarungsreden*), and a 'passion source'. This suggestion corresponds with the blocks of material found in the Gospel, namely, signs in the first twelve chapters, the passion narrative starting in chapter 18, and the discourses spread throughout the Gospel. (Although the focus will be on Bultmann, other corresponding arguments will be added to the following description since the aim is to illustrate how source critics argue their point.)

(a) According to Bultmann, the *'signs source'* – written in Greek with Hellenistic influences – consists of the seven signs in narrative form, limited to chapters 1–12 (2.1-11; 4.46-54; 5.2-9; 6.1-15; 6.16-21; 9.1-12?; 11.1-44 – the verses are approximate). Arguments in favour of the signs source are:

(i)   The numbering of the first two signs (2.11 and 4.54) that suggests the existence of a 'list'.
(ii) In 20.30-31 there is reference to the '*semeia*'/signs that were written down. These verses are then regarded as the conclusion of a (the) signs source and therefore proof of the original signs source.
(iii) Theological arguments based on the Christology presented in the signs are offered as supporting evidence. Bultmann suggests that this source was written by former disciples of John the Baptist as propaganda material for their faith. The aim was Christological: Jesus was described as the divine man (Gr. = *theios anēr*) who overwhelmed people with his miraculous nature. These signs were intended to evoke faith in Jesus based on his identity.

(b) The poetic style of the long discourses in the Gospel with its frequent antithetical parallelisms convinced Bultmann that a *'revelatory discourse source'* (a type of sayings source) lies behind the discourse material in the Gospel. Bultmann suggested that this source was taken from a context with strong Gnostic tendencies, the same context with which, for instance, the *Odes of Solomon*, Mandaean or Hermetic literature, or other second-century Gnostic material, could be associated. A major task of the Evangelist was to reformulate and recontextualize these Gnostic discourses by linking them to the Jesus-events.

Scholars are least convinced by this part of Bultmann's theory. No such Gnostic sources as Bultmann suggests can be proven to exist. They are hypothetical, which means that Bultmann's theological assumptions cannot be checked against concrete evidence. In any case, the sources Bultmann used to construct his argument post-date the Gospel material.

(c) The *passion narrative* contains parallels to the synoptics, although Bultmann maintained that the Johannine account was written independently from the synoptics. Nevertheless, it was suggested by some that John was dependent on Mark while others prefer Luke (Louvain school) as the source. Others suggest that John had access to some very old and reliable pre-Johannine traditions, which he integrated with his theology to form an independent narrative. Be that as it may, the original source the author used was reworked, formed into an independent narrative reflecting his own theology, and was redactionally enriched.

Bultmann suggested that each of these three above-mentioned sources came from a different socio-religious tradition. The Evangelist however integrated them effectively. This assumption by Bultmann forced him to interpret the theology of John in terms of Gnostic tendencies (i.e. aspects like light and darkness, life and death). According to Bultmann the original 'thrust' of the Gnostic source became the 'thrust' of the Gospel as such. It is little wonder that he sees the evangelist as one of the disciples of John the Baptist who was converted to Christianity and was strongly influenced by Gnosticism.

Fortna does not limit himself to a 'pure' signs source but prefers to talk about an original 'signs Gospel' that included a passion narrative, with 20.30-31 as its ending. This 'signs Gospel' was based on two sources that were merged, namely, signs and passion sources respectively. It was intended as a Gospel to the Jews as part of a missionary enterprise. Though it did not contain discourse material, the messianic nature of Jesus was the primary focus. This 'signs Gospel' (an independent Gospel on its own) served as the original source out of which the Evangelist created the Gospel we know today by adding some discourse material.

The existence of these or similar sources is heavily debated and even vigorously disputed. The differences in the process of composition suggested by two of the leading source critics above illustrates the hypothetical nature of this procedure. Many of the pro-source arguments are disputed on a detailed level and need not be considered here.

1.3.2 Editorial work resulting in tensions in the text

Source theories are used to explain the 'blocks' of material (a in Diagram 4.1, i.e. signs, discourses, and passion), but such approaches do not adequately explain the breaks and tensions in the text. For instance, how could it have happened that Jesus is in Jerusalem in chapter 5 and the next moment (in chapter 6) he is at the Sea of Galilee? This question becomes even more interesting when it is realized that if the chapters are reshuffled the problem can be eliminated: chapter 4 ends in Galilee – in chapter 6 Jesus continues his work in Galilee and in chapter 5 he goes to Jerusalem. By re-ordering the chapters this way (4-6-5) the tension is eliminated. These types of arguments prompted Bultmann to rearrange large sections of the Gospel (see his commentary) so that it could make more logical sense, according to him, of course.

But if one starts to rearrange the Gospel material as Bultmann did, one must first explain how such a disarrangement of the magnitude Bultmann suggested could have occurred in the first place. Bultmann argued that after the Gospel was written, the 'pages' somehow got disarranged – the different pages of the text were dislocated and mutilated. Since the original author was not present any longer to arrange them in the correct order, an ecclesiastical redactor or editor arranged them into the sequence we currently have. This, for instance, would explain the strange positioning of chapter 5 as noted above. Another explanation of the dislocation is that the Evangelist did not finish his Gospel himself – a disciple who had additional writings of the Evangelist at his disposal added the extra material freely to the already existing material, causing tensions and breaks. If we take the remark of Jesus in 14.31 that the disciples should get up and go but then he continues to talk for three chapters, such a solution could make sense. If chapters 15–17 are 'taken out' and 18.1 ('When Jesus had spoken these words, he went forth with his disciples across the Kidron valley …') follows, there would be a seamless transition in the narrative. This makes it plausible that chapters 15–17 could have been added later.

There are also theological tensions, for instance, with the sacraments: the Eucharist is not mentioned and Jesus and his disciples do not eat the Passover meal (13). Nevertheless 6.51c-58; 19.34b-35 seem to contain eucharistic language. The same applies to the presence of both realized and futuristic eschatological notions (5.28-29; 6.39, 40, 44, 54;

12.48). How can this be explained? Well, it is argued that the later 'ecclesiastical editor', who differed in his theology from the original Evangelist (i.e. on the Eucharist and eschatology), added this information in order to bring the theology of this Gospel more in line with the orthodox views of the surrounding Christianity at that later stage.

Bultmann suggested that it is the task of the present-day exegete to 'correct' the untidiness of the 'ecclesiastical editor' and rearrange the material so that we have it in the form it 'originally' was – that is, without tensions or sudden breaks. We should also separate the 'additions' of the 'ecclesiastical editor' from the text of the Gospel so that only the material reflecting the original theology of the Evangelist remains. Bultmann did this according to his own hermeneutical and interpretative strategy and embarked on a comprehensive restructuring of the Gospel, shifting even minor sections around, and thus 'constructed' the 'original Gospel', à la Bultmann.

It goes without saying that although Bultmann's work was very influential and dominated a significant part of the middle of the previous century his views were also severely criticized. The complexity of an elaborate process of composition such as he suggested was attributed by many to the creative and imaginative power of the exegete more than anything else. Serious engagement with Bultmann has highlighted difficulties with his approach that need not be discussed in detail here, since it is a wide-ranging debate (see Moody Smith or Frey). A few remarks should suffice, not to try and offer a detailed discussion, but merely to illustrate what type of methodological problems such source theories have:

(a) It is a question whether such an elaborate reconstruction of the 'original text' is justified, especially since the personal views of the exegete on the theology of John serve as criteria for judging what was 'original' and what not. The issue of present or future eschatology is, for instance, not a matter of literary criticism, but a matter of the theological opinion of the exegete on the content of the Johannine theology.

(b) The style and language of the different discourses and signs across the Gospel as a whole are so closely interrelated that it seems difficult to defend a theory that proposes sources that are completely unrelated, as Bultmann suggests. If the sources are completely independent, how did it happen that they utilize the same vocabulary and style?

(c) The existence of these sources is questionable because of the highly hypothetical nature of the arguments in their favour. None of these documents exists in writing, which makes it virtually impossible to verify theories or conclusions based on them. In the end one lands in circular argumentation by explaining the Gospel material in the light of hypothetical sources that were constructed from the Gospel itself.

(d) The dynamics of textual semantics are lost from sight (Culpepper). The current text is the only text we are sure really existed. Through the reconstruction of the text and especially the exclusion of certain parts of the text from the reconstruction, the structural semantics of the Gospel are changed. This results in a different flow of argument and therefore in a different meaning. This creates new problems of its own and such a rearrangement creates a new or different text nobody can prove ever existed, except in the mind of the person who suggests such a rearrangement.

There is little doubt that these are significant problems, but that, in spite of the hypothetical nature of these displacement theories, they will remain part of Johannine studies, especially because of the possibilities for creative exegesis.

1.4 The text is a 'seamless robe' or close knit unit

1.4.1 Reading the text as it is
Obviously the underlying assumption of the source or redactional theories is that the Johannine text as we have it is to a certain extent dysfunctional and does not make proper sense throughout. It 'needs help' from present-day interpreters to communicate properly. It is obviously assumed that the final editor was not able to create a functional text and in spite of the excellent literary features of this Gospel, the editor did not have the ability to smooth out these problems. Or, perhaps they did not bother him. However, many are convinced that the Gospel does make perfect sense as it now stands.

Another way of solving the apparent breaks and tensions is to explain them as an inherent part of the overall structure, style and composition of this Gospel. The so-called tensions should not be explained in terms of sources or redaction, but should rather be seen as logical and coherent parts of this Gospel. It is argued that the language and style of John's Gospel are so unified and homogeneous throughout the Gospel that it becomes difficult convincingly to distinguish different sources. The basic methodological principle becomes: only if the current shape of the text is demonstrably impossible on semantic, structural, or pragmatic levels, should it become justifiable to reorder the text, as Schnelle aptly points out. Put in another form, you need to have a very solid and unavoidable reason for reordering a text and excluding or altering certain sections.

The view that the text should be approached as a unit gained considerable ground during the last two decades of the previous century into the first decade of the present century. It is argued that the text we have is the only text that we are sure really existed. Schnelle points out that two methodological premises underlie this view:

(a) John's Gospel is regarded as a 'coherent text' with a 'high level of literary sophistication'. Each part of the Gospel forms a coherent and sensible part of the whole. The key for understanding the text is 'the intra-textual world of the entire Fourth Gospel' and not sources or motifs that reflect editorial work. Structural approaches (both on the level of narrative structures as well as structural analyses) are used to illustrate the coherence of sections of the Gospel or the Gospel as a whole.

(b) By taking the current form of the text seriously, attention is redirected from editors and underlying sources to the original author and his intentions. The major effort will not be to interpret the text in the light of the ideas found in different underlying sources (i.e. Gnostic, or Hellenistic, etc.), but will be primarily to understand the text in the light of the text itself.

Of course, it is a matter of interpretation (and explanation) whether the breaks and tensions mentioned above could be satisfactorily explained as a logical part of the current text of John's Gospel. (a) Detail problems should be solved text-internally. The Eucharist text in 6.51c-58 is not seen as a later addition, but rather as a conscious deepening and further development of the argumentation – not just Jesus as person, but now also his physical body are linked to the bread of life. This forms the high point of the whole argument in chapter 6. (b) Studies in consistency of style and vocabulary illustrate similarities on these levels throughout the Gospel. Networks of themes like kinship, kingship or temple imageries link different sections of the Gospel.

This weakens arguments in favour of different sources, since it must then be explained why different sources contain the same vocabulary and ideas.

Obviously, not all tensions and breaks are explained in an equally satisfactory way; for instance, the problems of the breaks in 14.31 and 20.30-31 remain difficult to solve. Some even feel that the problem with the Eucharistic material in 6.51c-58 is not solved yet. The question that should constantly be borne in mind is whether source or editorial theories are necessary to solve these problems. Could they not be solved intra-textually in a more satisfactory manner?

One serious warning must be sounded at this point: a concrete danger in only focusing on the text as a completed whole is that the historical dimensions of the text may be overlooked. What is required is a balanced approach. It must be remembered that a text and its history are linked. By constructing a history of the community based on the text and its history, a framework is created within which theological interpretation is made. By just focusing on the text itself this historical dimension might easily be neglected or even entirely lost.

1.4.2 Some exegetical approaches resulting from focus on the text as it is

Let us now move on to a different but related issue, namely, the methodological approaches used to interpret the text as we have it. The results of these approaches are often used to motivate the unity of the text, since the different literary phenomena are spread throughout the Gospel, which weakens the arguments for different sources. The focus falls on the synchronic, literary nature of the text.

With *source*-orientated approaches, the emphasis falls on the sources behind the text. *Text*-orientated approaches, on the other hand, focus on the text as *text*. The object of study is usually the final text as we have it, focusing on the structure and literary characteristics of the text. The emphasis can even shift to the reader of the text. The interpretative experiences of the different readers of the text are studied in the different reader-orientated approaches. Let us take a brief look at the essence of some of these approaches, focusing on the text and its readers.

(a) Different *structural approaches* to the text may be distinguished, depending on the criteria that are used in determining a structure of the text. Examples are: (i) There are efforts to discover the general structure of the Gospel. Some suggest that the Gospel is structured *chiastically* (A–B–C–B¹–A¹). Others use signals in the Gospel, like the structure of the travels of Jesus, or the different feasts in the Gospel, to structure the content of the Gospel. There are also efforts to structure smaller sections of the text according to chiasms, parallelisms, repetitions, etc. For instance, in John 1.1-5 we find a staircase parallelism: Word/Word-God/God-life/life-light/light-darkness/darkness. Parallelisms and repetitions abound (for instance, 15.4 or 10). These efforts vary in feasibility and functionality.

Narratology is also used as a means to structure the text. Culpepper was instrumental in drawing attention to the development of the plot of the Gospel (outlined in the Prologue – 1.9-13. The rejection vs. the acceptance of Jesus forms the plot according to him). The characteristics of the different (A)actors, their relations, the use of space and time in the Gospel, and the development of the plot are all investigated in detail. Unique features of John's narrative, like having long speeches where there is no real 'narrative action', are pointed out. Although these methods still form an integral part of the exegesis of the Johannine literature, their popularity has waned recently.

(b) *Reception theories* but also *reaction* (or ideological) *theologies* focus on the influence of the reader on the understanding of the text. The latter include feminist or revolutionary readings of the text. In such cases the text is read from a specific perspective (for instance, from the perspective of feminism or oppression) and the results of the reading process specifically related to that particular perspective. A feminist reading will *inter alia* give special attention to the Samaritan woman, who is the first missionary to the Samaritans (4.27-30), or Mary Magdalene, who is the first witness to the risen Christ (20.18), Jesus' special relation to Martha and Mary (11.1-6) or the way Jesus' mother is introduced into the family of God (19.26-27). These themes will then be brought to the foreground of the text.

Reader-response theories, on the other hand, focus on a reader's views that consciously and significantly impact on the understanding of the message of the text. The creative process of understanding receives special attention. The magnitude of personal applications of Johannine material underlines the communicative power of the Johannine texts (especially because of the strong figurative nature of the material), as well as the significant role readers play. This forms part of the enigma and the popularity of the Johannine text.

(c) Some approaches focus on the *rhetorical* and *stylistic* features of the text. The Johannine writings, especially the Gospel, are known for distinct stylistic features. These features are usually discussed under style or literary characteristics, but they also play a significant role in influencing the reader.

These stylistic features contribute to the *performative* nature of the text (that is to say, the text wants to do something concrete to its reader). The reader is drawn into the dynamics of the text. The text 'performs' in the reader and the reader performs on account of the text; or put differently, the reader reads the text and the text reads the reader.

The performative nature of the text was already discussed in chapter 1 and only a brief recap is necessary. The statement of the purpose in

20.30-31 says: 'these (the Gospel and its signs) are written so that you may (come to) believe …' Jesus is no longer physically present with believers, but the Gospel is there as a replacement of his 'presence'. Those who read it will be confronted with the living 'Jesus' through the text, since the text becomes the substitute for the physical Jesus.

Obviously the pure message of the narrative carries performative potential, but that is not all. The way the material is presented – that is, the style of the Gospel – also invites readers to participate. This also makes the text performative – once readers answer to the text's invitation to participate, they get involved in the narrative world and can then hardly escape the performative power of the Gospel. They become 'actors' in the narrative in their own right.

What follows is a brief description of some of the major *stylistic* features in the Gospel.

(i) *Wordplay*: John has a flexible way of using words. One should never assume you know what he means with a particular choice of words. Constant surprises await the careful reader. In this way the reader remains alert and involved. A few examples of his flexible use of words now follow:

- *Double meaning:* Often the exact meaning of a word in a particular context is difficult to determine, since more than one meaning is possible and seems to be implied. In 1.5 we have the following expression, 'the darkness did not *katelaben* it'. This Greek word can be translated as 'overcome/overpower' or 'comprehend/grasp'. Both translations make perfect sense and most probably both are implied. In 3.3 the Greek word *anōthen* in the sentence 'unless one is born *anōthen*, one cannot …' may be translated as 'from above' or 'again'. No definite choice can be made here either. The word is used with an intended double meaning.
- The *same word* is used with *different meanings* throughout the Gospel. The Greek word *kosmos* may, for instance, be used for the world (as creation), the people of this world, or evil people of this world, depending on the context.
- *Different words* are used with the *same meaning*. The words *agapaō* and *fileō* are both translated as 'love'. Although there are efforts by some to distinguish between godly and human love these words basically both mean the same thing, 'to love'. (In 16.27 God's love is referred to by using *fileō* – the word some claim to be human love.)

(ii) *Misunderstanding:* Often listeners misunderstand Jesus, and this of course gives him a chance to correct their misunderstanding by revealing the truth. This is a performative technique, since the reader usually knows the correct answer and therefore immediately recognizes the stupidity of the person who misunderstands. By acknowledging that Jesus gives the correct answer the reader identifies him or herself with that particular answer. For instance, Nicodemus misunderstands Jesus when Jesus says that he must be spiritually born again. He thinks Jesus talks about going into the womb of his mother again (3.4). This gives Jesus a chance to elaborate (3.3-8). The Samaritan woman also misunderstands Jesus when he says he will give her water (4.11). Jesus then explains to her what the living water is (4.10-14).

(iii) *Irony* and *paradox:* Irony occurs when persons say something in ignorance, without realizing that what they say is actually true, usually not in the way they intend it to be. The events of the cross are soaked in irony. For instance, the crowd claims that a blasphemer like Jesus should be put to death, because he is an evildoer (18.30), but *they* are actually the evildoers who deserve death. Ironically, they judge themselves. The high priest says that it would be better to have one man die for the people than to have the whole nation destroyed (11.50). Ironically, Jesus did die to save the nation or family of God, although the high priest did not realize the truth of his words and obviously did not intend it the way it turned out.

Paradox is a statement that seems contradictory, yet it is true. The crowd accuses Jesus of making himself Son of God while he is not and therefore he should die. Paradoxically for them, Jesus is indeed the Son of God (19.7). Through irony and paradox statements are intensified and emphasized with the reader. When the crowds blame Jesus for making himself the Son of God, the reader immediately sees the paradox: he *is* the Son of God, and by acknowledging that, a statement of confession is implied with the reader, even if it is implicit. Obviously, any real reader can reject the truth of this statement, but while the reader is part of the narrative world of the text, the statement must be upheld.

(iv) *Imagery, metaphors* and *symbolism* are basic stylistic tools in the Gospel. Jesus is the vine (15.1), the gate for the sheep (10.7), the bread of life (6.35), or the way (14.6). Believers are born again and become part of the spiritual family of God (figurative or metaphorical language). Kinship, temple and kingship language create some of the major imageries that form networks of figurative language through the Gospel as a whole, as became apparent when the theological analysis of the message of the Gospel was made in a previous chapter.

(v) *Forensic language* contributes to the performative nature of the Gospel. By using forensic language, the author creates a 'court case scenario' in which the reader is drawn into the narrative to form part of the jury. The reader must eventually be the judge of what is right or wrong. For instance, based on the witnesses Jesus calls on his behalf in 5.30-47 there cannot be any doubt with the 'jury' that he comes from the Father. Chapter 8.13 starts with words like 'testimony' or 'testify' laying the forensic foundation for what follows. Jesus and his opponents engage in serious arguments, the way one would argue in an ancient court. Eventually the reader must be the judge. The discussion between the blind man and the Pharisees in chapter 9 is also forensic in nature. Eventually the blind man is judged and thrown out of the synagogue. The reader can follow the argument, which is clearly won by the blind man, who is then treated unjustly. Again the reader becomes involved in judging the outcome. In this way, the text becomes performative, actively drawing the reader into the narrative world of the text.

Reading John's literature is an adventure, because of the complexity and richness of the text. There is constantly a story behind the story, a playfulness with irony and paradox, imageries and metaphors opening the transcendent world in a simple, but nevertheless complex way, enticing the reader with wordplay to intellectually partake in the narrative, correcting misunderstandings, recognizing *double entendre*, or the different meanings of the same word. It is indeed a text in which the baby can bathe, because of its simplicity, but in which the elephant can drown, because of its complexity. This is where the excitement of reading John comes to light.

This brings us to the next issue when dealing with the Johannine documents. We have seen that the Johannine documents have unique literary and stylistic characteristics that give their own flavour to the Jesus narrative. This unique presentation of the message distinguishes it from other related Christian narratives. This raises interesting questions, like where these Johannine documents came from, or who wrote them, when and why? These questions into the origins of the Gospel and Letters ask our attention in the next chapter.

5

Where Does John's Gospel Come From?

The Johannine Gospel and Letters are firmly embedded into ancient Christian literature with strong roots in the Old Testament. But who was behind the composition of the Gospel and Letters? Was the author an eyewitness and when did he write them? What caused the unevenness in the text (see previous chapter) and what does that tell us about the process of composition?

These questions are part of the larger Johannine puzzle. Again it should be said that decisions made on this level will impact on how one should understand other issues like socio-cultural influences on the Gospel, the history of development of the ideas, decisions on the relationship with the synoptics, and so forth. In what follows, we will follow the development of the arguments on authorship step by step.

1. Who wrote the Gospel?

1.1 John, the son of Zebedee

Until recently, it was accepted that John, the son of Zebedee, was the author of this Gospel. These arguments were based on the oldest evidence that dates back to the first quarter of the second century.

Our ancient point of orientation is an important second-century church father, Irenaeus (ca. 180 CE). He wrote a book called *Adversus Haereses* (Against the Heretics) in which he identifies John, the son of Zebedee, as the author of the Gospel according to John. After referring to the authors of the other three Gospels, he makes the following remark in III.1.2: 'Afterwards, John, the disciple of the Lord, who also had leaned upon His breast, did himself publish a Gospel during his residence at Ephesus in Asia.' This idea was confirmed by Theophilus, sixth bishop of Antioch (died

181[8] CE), who also ascribed this Gospel to John (perhaps the son of Zebedee?), as well as Polucrates of Ephesus (190 CE). By the end of the second century this Gospel was firmly linked to the name of John, even in the Canon of Muratori (179–200 CE). This placed the origin of John's Gospel firmly in the hands of an eyewitness from the first century. For many centuries, until the emergence of critical studies in the eighteenth century, this was the general consensus among scholars.

The internal evidence from the Gospel seems to support arguments in favour of John as author. The only apparent reference to the author of the Gospel is in John 21.20, 24 where the author is identified with the Beloved Disciple. According to John 21.2, 20-24 he could either have been one of the sons of Zebedee or one of the two anonymous disciples who were fishing with the group. The strange reservedness about the names of the sons of Zebedee in John's Gospel (John is not mentioned) is seen as an argument in favour of linking one of them, namely John, to the Beloved Disciple, as a special form of identification. This means that John, son of Zebedee, must have lived to a ripe old age to be able to write the Gospel at the end of the first century. There is traditional support for this. Irenaeus (Eusebius, *Ecclesiastical History* 3.23.1-4) indeed claims that John lived into the reign of Trajan (98-117 CE). However, in spite of these arguments it is not possible to identify the Beloved Disciple with absolute certainty with a particular historical person. Nevertheless, by the end of the second century the Beloved Disciple was associated with John, son of Zebedee, although in the long run this position could not be absolutely sustained.

1.2 Different Johns?

In 1792 Evanson shocked the existing consensus by arguing that due to the discrepancies between the four Gospels, this Gospel could not have been written by John, the disciple of Jesus. He also dismissed the claim by Irenaeus that John was the son of Zebedee as apologetics against the Gnostics. Irenaeus just attributed the Gospel to a disciple or apostle in order to strengthen his case and did not present historically verifiable evidence in doing so.

But, if John, son of Zebedee, did not write the Gospel, who did? A search for possible 'authors' started and different names were suggested, of whom a few are mentioned.

(a) In the search for *other* '*Johns*' another 'John' (not the son of Zebedee) was discovered. Irenaeus states (*Haer.* 5.33.4; quoted by Eusebius, *Hist. Eccl.* 3.39.1-4) that Papias was 'a hearer of John and a companion of Polycarp'. He further mentions that Papias refers to two persons, both named 'John' – the one John is linked to the apostles while the other was called 'John, the elder' (Gr. = *presbuteros*). Since both are called disciples, some scholars see them as one and the same person, John, the son of Zebedee. Others distinguish them by saying that the reference is to two separate people, implying that there was another influential John, called the elder, who could also have been the author of this Gospel and Letters. To complicate the matter further, there is a third John, John Mark (Acts 12.12). All three could have been an author of the Letters, and even this Gospel.

(b) Another suggestion is *Lazarus*. In 11.5 it is explicitly said that Jesus loves Lazarus. This is enough to convince some scholars that Lazarus is indeed the *Beloved Disciple* (13.23) and therefore the author of the Gospel (21.2, 20-24). In any case, the rumour that the Beloved Disciple will not die (21.23) fits this scenario, since it might be that people thought that of Lazarus after Jesus raised him from the grave.

(c) There are others who maintain that the author should remain *anonymous*. One cannot be sure who the author really was. References to the Beloved Disciple do not help that much, since it is difficult to identify him with a specific historical figure. This leads to the only real option: a broad description of the author(s) as perhaps, or perhaps not, one of the twelve, but at least part of the Johannine community. This is as far as they would like to go in identifying a specific author.

John, son of Zebedee, of course, stayed a popular candidate based on the ancient tradition. The way his role is viewed however changed over time from being the person who physically wrote down the Gospel to the source of the content of the Gospel. He is often not seen as the physical writer, but as a mediating figure behind the Gospel from whom the Johannine material and tradition originated. Somebody else (an anonymous figure or figures) wrote down the material based on his witness. How this could have happened is a matter of speculation. Some ascribe virtually all the authority to John while others regard his influence as being somewhat limited. An example of such a suggestion is, for instance, that John passed his notes on to others who reworked the notes with a greater or lesser measure of freedom.

1.3 Not a single author but a process of development

In the previous century the idea of the composition of the Gospel radically changed. Instead of searching for a single author, attention shifted to the possibility that the Gospel developed over a longer period of time and involved several different authors/editors. Creative involvement by several people (i.e. authors, writers, redactors) at different stages in the development of the Gospel material now became the focus of the investigation rather than the position of a single author. It is argued that the material found in John's Gospel was entrusted to the Johannine community (with different writers and redactors involved) who had an authoritative figure (like John, the son of Zebedee) or figures to vouch for the authenticity of this Gospel.

1.3.1 The Gospel as a 'two-level drama' – where the Jesus-events and the community situation are integrated

The important book of J. Louis Martyn (1968) gave significant impetus to the idea of community involvement in the composition of the Gospel. However, more was at stake than just authorship. The historical framework within which the Johannine Christians functioned was now at stake. Questions were asked such as how and why such a group could produce such a document. What were the forces and influences behind the composition of the Gospel? In this way, different issues like authorship, time of writing, the situation of the community that produced the Gospel are all integrated. The answer on the one question will have a direct impact on what one should conclude about the others. For instance, a late date of composition will allow for a long period of development and will imply more community involvement, and so on. Let us take Louis Martyn's argument as an example of this complex interrelatedness.

Martyn took his cue from the signs of conflict between the disciples of Jesus and their Jewish opponents (15.18–16.4). The three references to the disciples of Jesus being put out of the synagogue (Gr. = *aposynagogos* – 9.22; 12.42; 16.2) are of particular importance. He pinpoints the story of the healing of the blind man who was eventually excluded from the synagogue (9.22) as a 'double story'. Not only does it tell about the healing of the blind man but it is also a reflection on the situation in which the later Johannine Christians found themselves. Because the blind man testified about Jesus and refused to deny his faith he was thrown out of the synagogue. The same happened to the Johannine Christians for the same reasons, Martyn argues.

But the question was: when did this expulsion from the synagogue take place? Martyn concludes that the story of the blind man in 9.22 actually reflects events that took place at the time the Eighteen Benedictions (*Birkath ha-Minim*), the daily prayers of the Jews, were formulated in Jamnia by Rabban Gamaliel II in the 80s of the first century. The twelfth prayer contained negative remarks about non-Jews (called insolents or heretics). Martyn links this prayer to Christians and interprets it as a sign of the split between Christians and Jews at that stage. Up to that point the Johannine Christians were still part of the synagogue system. Because of their confession of Jesus – like the blind man – they were expelled. This fortified their position, and from then on they claimed that Jesus was the only way. This led to further persecution and even death (16.2). What we read in 9.22 is therefore a 'two-level story': it is a reflection of later events, embedded in a miracle story of Jesus that took place in an earlier period.

This was an important suggestion, since it meant that the content of the Gospel no longer simply dealt with the narrative of Jesus in Galilee or Jerusalem alone, but also reflected the situation of the Johannine Christians decades later in other places. By telling the story of Jesus in this particular way, the Jesus-events are integrated with the history of these Christians dating from decades later – truly a *two-level drama*. This integration of the Jesus story with the concrete experiences of the Johannine Christians developed over decades – the Jesus-events took place in more or less 30 CE and the Gospel was only finalized in its present form more or less during the last decade of the first century – a period of sixty years.

By investigating the theological or even narratological characteristics, an idea of what happened in the community could be formed. The fair assumption is that John's narrative would reflect all the significant events that took place in the community and the Gospel is then read from such a perspective. Events, like introducing Samaritans into their group, being expelled from the synagogues, the development from a low to a high Christology, reflected different 'stages' in the history of the Johannine Christians. The contents of the Gospel indeed reflect the historical dynamics of that community and the contents appear to relate to, and result from, their life, worship, and instruction.

Excursus: *Martyn's suggestions:* This issue of the Benedictions as indicative of the breaking point between Judaism and Christianity is disputed, and it is assumed to be a weak point in Martyn's argument. However, his suggestion of a two-level drama still enjoys wide acceptance, although it is also criticized. Hägerland (2003), for instance, argues that there are no parallels for the two-level drama in ancient literature. Articles in Bauckham (1998) also argue for a wider audience for the Gospels, which implies that such a narrow focus on one community as basis for a Gospel becomes less probable.

1.3.2 The Gospel developed in stages under community influence

The realization that the Johannine group was most probably involved in the formation and growth of the Gospel confronted the ardent researcher with major new questions. Who were these Christians? How and why were they involved in the formation of the Gospel as we have it today? The history of the community was now inseparably linked to the history of the formation of the Gospel. It was no longer possible to address the one issue without considering the other. The different issues addressed in the Gospel reflect different stages of development of the community. By looking at what 'happens in the Gospel' the historical dynamics within the community can be reconstructed. If nothing would have happened in the community the history of the development of the Gospel would also have been static and the other way round. As soon as something significant happened, it was reflected in the Gospel material.

As part of the process of the construction of the history of this community, the Johannine Letters also became significant. Assumed to be part of the documents of this community, they also reflect what happened at certain stages within the community. In this way the picture of the community we have in the Gospel is broadened and enriched by the information from the Letters. A more comprehensive description of the community and its development therefore becomes much more possible.

Thus, in the middle of the twentieth century a major focus in Johannine research was the nature and development of the Johannine community. Many players took to the field and played complicated and speculative games in order to reconstruct the history of the Johannine community. In Germany Richter (1975) used different Christological positions (i.e. the Mosaic-prophet Christians; Son of God Christians; docetic and antidocetic Christians) to distinguish between the different stages of development of the Gospel. Each of these Christian groups had a specific influence on the formation of the Gospel and gave the content a specific slant. In England Lindars (1971) offered an elaborate theory of different stages of development where the oral traditions took the form of homilies, which were later collected by the community. In this way the formation of the Gospel started. As a result of the Jewish relations that turned sour other material was added and the order of the material was rearranged to form a Gospel. To this revised Gospel later 'post-Johannine' additions were made to create the final Gospel as we have it today.

However, it was the construction of the history of the community by the American, Raymond Brown (1979 and 2003) that became the most widely accepted, and most influential in this area of scholarship and research.

Brown originally (1979) distinguished five stages in the composition of the Gospel but later reduced it to three stages (2003), without changing the essence of his view. His most recent suggestion of three stages of development for the Gospel plus a fourth for the Letters will now briefly receive our attention. Note the way in which several different issues, namely, development of ideas, dependence upon sources, historical events in the community, date, authors and editors involved, are all integrated and become interdependent.

Stage 1: 'Origin in the public ministry or activity of Jesus of Nazareth' Companions, travelling with Jesus, memorized the words and deeds of Jesus, providing the raw 'Jesus material' to early Christians. This availed a body of traditional material from which both John and the synoptics sprang. One of the disciples of Jesus, later known as the Beloved Disciple, shaped and preserved the Jesus material within his particular framework and perspective. He most probably had former links with the disciples of John the Baptist. 'Jews of different religious backgrounds could have comprehended Jesus differently and appreciated different aspects of his message', Brown says (2003: 66). Some of the material was similar to that of the synoptics (which explains links with synoptic material), but obviously there were also differences. The development of a specific Johannine perspective within the community therefore goes back to authentic and traditional 'Jesus material' though coloured by the perspective of the Beloved Disciple. The Johannine community therefore has its roots firmly in Jewish Christianity.

Stage 2: 'Proclaiming Jesus in the post-resurrection context of community history'
A period now followed during which the Gospel was not yet physically written down. The traditions about Jesus (*Stage 1*) were kept 'alive' in and indeed motivated the life and worship of the Christian communities, especially in light of their experience of the resurrection. During this period the 'Jesus material' was specifically developed to fit Johannine patterns by the community, most probably under the influence and guidance of a principal teacher, who most probably was the Beloved Disciple.

Brown utilizes the differences with the synoptics (i.e. the presence of the Samaritans, the conflict with the Jews on the basis of the high Christology) as a methodological tool to construct the dynamics of the unique development of the Johannine community. The following, for instance, are significant:

(a)   The presence and membership of the *Samaritans* in the Johannine community are unique to John (4; 8.48). As part of the Johannine community they co-determined the community's identity. This explains:

- the significant role of Moses in this Gospel, since Moses was a key figure in Samaritan religion;
- the strong anti-Jewish language in this Gospel, which would not be strange in a Samaritan context.

(b) The influence of Moses traditions had a notable impact on the *Christology* of the Gospel, since Moses was a central figure in the Samaritan religion and was traditionally linked with personified divine Wisdom. In describing Jesus in contrast to Moses, a high Christology (surpassing the synoptics) resulted, since Christians had to show that Jesus was even more important than Moses. To underline this, use was made of 'God language' (1.1; 20.28) that included the idea of pre-existence.

(c) During this second stage the high Christology resulted in conflict with the Jews (5.18; 10.33). The conflict ended in the expulsion of the Johannine community from the *synagogue* by the Jewish authorities (9.22; 12.34; 16.2). This might explain the forensic language in the Gospel, since there must have been considerable arguments between the Johannine community and the Jewish authorities. This had the effect that the Johannine community no longer thought of themselves as 'Jews', but developed their own unique identity.

Stage 3: 'The writing of the Gospel'
Writing down this living tradition by real living people followed. But who were they? Although it is difficult to prove conclusively, as Brown acknowledges, it does not seem plausible that a single author was responsible for the Gospel from beginning to end. Brown also doubts whether the Beloved Disciple – who was the formative figure in Stage 2 and was most probably dead by now – was involved in the process of writing the material down in its present form. This was left to two of the followers of the Beloved Disciple: an evangelist and a redactor. An evangelist wrote the body of the Gospel (not as a pre-Gospel text, but as an entire Gospel). He selected and edited the available material according to the needs of the Johannine community and arranged it into the current form of the Gospel. It is also possible that he made smaller adjustments later due to changing circumstances within the community. The refined literary style with the lengthy discourses and intriguing narratives come from his hand.

A redactor later made some additions, though not corrections. Brown argues that there was still some Johannine material available from Stages 1 and 2 that the evangelist did not use. The nature of this material was similar to that already contained in the Gospel.

Methodologically this implies that the theory of 'development' (i.e. less developed and more developed theological ideas) is not a trustworthy criterion to distinguish between the work of the evangelist and that of the redactor. Awkwardness and duplication of material serve as better criteria. Examples of redactional work, according to Brown, are 3.31-36; 12.44-50; 6.51-58 next to 6.35-50; the Prologue (1.1-18) and the Epilogue (21). Even chapters 15–17 come into consideration as the work of the redactor.

However, after the Fourth Gospel was written it did not signal the end of the history or activity of the community. This is evident from the existence of the Johannine Letters (obviously assuming they chronologically follow the Gospel). Brown argues that a close link exists between the Gospel and Letters, so much so that most units in the Letters show a conscious reflection on Gospel material.

From the *Letters* it becomes evident that there were serious differences of opinion in the Johannine community, which eventually resulted in schism (1 Jn 2.18-21; 2 Jn 10). Apparently, due to the developments during Stages 2 and 3, the community closed their ranks and hardened their position, especially in connection with the uniqueness and status of Jesus. These discussions about Jesus led to differences of opinion within the community and eventually to schism. In this debate at least two groups may be distinguished, namely, those who interpreted the Christological material in the Gospel as 'naive docetism' (Käsemann) and those who favoured a more orthodox view, namely, that Jesus was both divine and human. He gave those who believe in him eternal life and expected them to love one another. This conflict of opinion within the community invited the writing of 1 and 2 John, where the author favoured and supported the more orthodox view. The Letters of John addressed the specific conflicts within the community by reshaping the material of the Gospel. Like the Gospel, the Letters also combined the message of Jesus with the life and history of the community.

Unlike the Gospel, the Letters were most probably written by a single author over a brief period of time without any mentionable development or redaction. It is not clear whether the same person wrote the three letters, since the Presbyter mentioned in 2 and 3 John as the author might not have been the author of 1 John – he is, of course, not explicitly mentioned as the author.

In this way Brown tried to present a comprehensive view of the development of the Gospel that led to its composition. Many variations and speculations on this view followed, but the essence remained largely the same.

> **Excursus:** *Exegetical advantages that arise from a multilayered approach:* What would the exegetical gain be from a theory that the material contained in the Gospel grew through different stages? It is assumed by many exegetes that the Gospel was composed through different stages and this can be detected by tracing the development of, for instance, Christological expressions (from a low to a high Christology) or expressions related to the death of Christ and its significance (from primitive descriptions to expressions that contain a high level of interpretation). This 'reading behind the text', using expressions in the text to deduce historical developments behind the text, results in different 'theologies' that can be identified in the Gospel, namely, the theology of the original evangelist or the theology(ies) of the later editor(s). Ironically the 'stage theory' of Brown is often cited as the basis on which the different levels are identified, although Brown (2003: 82) is quite sceptical of the validity of such a procedure.

One brief *example* should suffice to illustrate the general procedure of such exegetical approaches. De Boer (1996) proposes four understandings of the death of Jesus, based on the distinguishable layers of four successive editions of the Gospel and Letters.

Three major periods in the history of the Gospel prompted three different perspectives on the death of Jesus.

(a) Initially the Johannine group found themselves within the framework of the Jewish synagogue. There the death of Jesus as *Messiah* was questioned and the Johannine groups had to emphasize the fulfilment of Scripture, with the resurrection as the climax of the divine signs ('Signs source'). In this way they relativized the scandal of the death of the Messiah.

(b) A major crisis, namely, the *rejection* of the Johannine group from the *synagogue*, influenced the second perspective on the death of Jesus – what Jesus did is explicitly linked to God, the Father, as was clear from his mission. He was sent on a mission by the Father and had to return. His death was his obedient return to the Father after completing his mission. Its salvific significance played no real role.

(c) The crisis with the Jewish opponents escalated and the Johannine community now started to experience hatred and persecution. Because of the hardship, the death of Jesus is now positively described as *glory*. Jesus vindicates his suffering followers by judging the prince of this world. Johannine Christians should therefore see their own suffering as glorious.

(d) Then came the schism in the Johannine community (6.60-71; 1 Jn 2.19). Since the schism was Christological in nature, it now became necessary to emphasize sacrificial aspects of the death of Jesus. Terms like water, blood, flesh, and expiation were now introduced to express the significance of the death of Jesus.

This illustrates how the 'layered approach' influences exegetical procedures. Different perspectives are distinguished and to a certain extent separated based on different stages of development of the Gospel and Letters.

1.3.3 The authorship of the Letters

Brown presented a plausible theory about the place and authorship of the Letters, but it is obviously not the only one.

The easiest way to deal with the authorship of the Letters is by starting with 2 and 3 John where the author is explicitly mentioned. In the first verse of both 2 and 3 John the author calls himself the 'elder' (Greek = *presbuteros*), leading to the conclusion that 2 and 3 John have been written by the same person (called 'John, the elder'). The authorship of 1 John is then linked to the other two letters based on similarities in style, vocabulary and concepts. The fact that 1 John was most probably a circular letter, in the form of a homily, might be the reason why there is no reference to an author like there is in 2 and 3 John. Not all scholars agree with this conclusion on the authorship. What is certain is that no clear consensus exists on this issue.

There are defenders of the view that 1 John was written by John, the son of Zebedee. They argue that the Semitic character of the Letter, as well as the reference in 1 John 1.1-4 to the author being an eyewitness, points to John, the son of Zebedee as the author. However, the argument in favour of this position rests on assumptions that the Beloved Disciple was responsible for writing the Gospel and that he indeed was John, the son of Zebedee. This weakens the argument. Apart from that the theological differences between the Gospel and 1 John, for instance, the eschatology, the idea of expiation, or references to the antichrists, also cast doubts over the assumption that the author(s) of the Gospel and of the Letters were the same. Some even think that the author of 1 John might have been one of the editors/redactors during the latter stages of the composition of the Gospel.

Following the composition of the Letters it seems that the community split up and dissolved, since we do not have evidence of such a group in the early second century. The group that was identified as the 'opponents' in the Letters most probably moved into Gnostic environments (if we consider the role of the Gospel in Gnostic material), while the other group seems to have merged with the larger early Christian movement of the time. This signalled the end of the Johannine community, but not of Johannine influence. The Gospel played a major role in the history of the Church. It started as early as the writings of Ignatius of Antioch (110 CE) and continued during the time of the church fathers up to today.

The discussion above illustrates how different issues related to the Gospel and Letters are interwoven. Authorship cannot be separated from the history of the Johannine community, which again is linked to the history of the composition of these documents. Issues like the dates of composition or reasons why these documents were written cannot be considered in isolation, since they are all directly influenced by the view one takes on the composition of the Gospel and Letters. One must always be aware of what effect a decision taken on one issue will have on the others.

2. When were the Gospel and Letters composed and where?

2.1 A date? Which date?

The insight that the *Gospel* was constructed over a period of (many) years changed the way questions of date or place of origin are dealt with. Since not one person but many were involved over a longer period of time at perhaps more than one location, it changes the manner in which one settles upon a date of writing. When the issue of the 'date' is addressed one must be clear what one is aiming to address. Most certainly one should not picture a single author sitting in a room somewhere on a specific date writing a Gospel. The process was much more complicated than that.

If one is interested in the whole period of composition (including the oral tradition), the 'date of composition' would be somewhere between the emergence of the earliest tradition, probably just before 40 CE, and the final redaction at the turn of the first century, which leaves one with 60 years of composition history. If one favours a 'stages approach' one could give dates for the start and end of each stage, which will leave one with several dates, ranging from before 40 CE to the turn of the first century. One can even limit oneself to the written process (from sources being written down to final redaction), which will leave one with a shorter period of time. If one is interested in the final version of the Gospel as we have it today, a fixed date at the turn of the century could be given.

In the light of these possibilities let us first focus on the date of the completion of the *final version* as we have it today. To answer this question one should ask: what could be the earliest (*terminus post quem*) and what the latest date of composition (*terminus ante quem*)? Answering these two questions provides a framework within which a more specific date could be set.

(a) *The latest possible date* (terminus ante quem). During the previous two centuries there was a tendency to date John's Gospel even as late as 150–160 CE based on arguments such as:

- The alleged dependence on the synoptics: it was argued that John's Gospel could only have been written after the last synoptic Gospel was completed and had sufficient time to filter through to varied Christian groups.
- It is also argued that it took a long time (several decades) for the high Christology as well as the independent tradition of this Gospel to develop.

These types of arguments, making use of Hegelian developmental or related theories, are however no longer regarded as trustworthy analytical criteria for determining the age of ideas, since a variety of views coexisted from early on in early Christian thought, not requiring long periods of development. It is indeed difficult to put a stopwatch on the development of ideas. When circumstances or situations change, development or rapid change could take place rather quickly, or *vice versa*.

However, nothing beats solid evidence. The publication in 1935 of the Rylands Papyrus (P^{52}) containing fragments of John 18.31-33, 37-38 proved the presence of the Gospel of John in Egypt as early as the first part of the second century. Papyrus Egerton 2 (about 150 CE) also discovered in Egypt, attributes equal authority to all four Gospels – a consensus that must have needed some time to be reached after the individual Gospels were written. Although it is difficult to quantify the time it would take for documents to reach Egypt from somewhere else (perhaps Syria or Asia Minor) or to quantify the time it would take for the four Gospels to be attributed similar authority, most scholars feel comfortable with 100–115 CE as a cut-off point for the final composition of John's Gospel.

(b) *The earliest possible date* (terminus post quem). The Johannine *tradition* (especially the oral tradition) at least dates back to the period before the fall of the temple in 70 CE and might even go so far back as 40 CE Our question is, however, not about the development of the tradition, but about the earliest possible date for writing down the Gospel as we have it today. There are several possibilities, and they are closely linked with authorship:

(i)   If the final author were an eyewitness of the Jesus-events, it would mean a date within the first century, since it is unlikely that an eyewitness would live into the second century.

(ii) If the author knew Palestine and its history and referred to places there as if they were still intact (there is, for instance, no reference to the destruction of the temple in 70 CE), it could mean that the time of writing corresponds to an early period where the author was still in Palestine.

(iii) Add to this the fact that some scholars are of the opinion that the author did not know the synoptics. This could imply that the Gospel predates the synoptics, since the author is not aware of them.

(iv) An argument that may support either of these arguments, depending on how it is interpreted, is based on the conflict between the synagogue and the Johannine Christians. Martyn linked this conflict, and especially the expulsion from the synagogue, to the *Berkath ha Minim* of the mid-80s soon after the Council of Jamnia. This would suggest a later date. However, this view has come under considerable criticism. This allows for proposing an earlier date, since conflicts between Christian and Jewish groups in different areas did occur earlier than the 80s and perhaps the author could refer to them.

With arguments like these some try to push the earliest date back to before 70 CE (see especially Robinson). However, the conflict with the Jewish opponents and the eventual expulsion from the synagogue (9.22; 12.42; 16.20) makes such an early date dubious. Even more telling is the reference to the death of the Beloved Disciple in 21.18-19. Peter died as a martyr in the 60s after which the Beloved Disciple apparently still lived for a while. This leaves us somewhere in the 70s CE as the earliest date.

The time framework within which John's Gospel was given its final form therefore lies between the 70s and the middle of the second decade of the second century. Again it can be said most scholars feel comfortable with a final date within the last decade of the first century (90–100), even though pinpointing it precisely is not possible.

But what about the *Letters*? When were they written? The dating of the Letters is obviously closely related to the Gospel and the history of the community. Two possibilities should be considered seriously. Firstly, that the Letters were written after the final composition of the Gospel as a reaction against misunderstandings about the Christology found in the

Gospel. The date of the composition of the Letters would then be shortly after the Gospel – between 95 and 100 CE, obviously depending on when one dates the final composition of the Gospel. However, if the Letters predate the Gospel, the date of composition may be earlier, also depending on the estimated date of final composition of the Gospel. Then a date somewhere in the late 80s or early 90s of the first century may be a realistic possibility.

2.2 Place or places? The place of origin of the Gospel and Letters

Where were the Gospel and Letters written? It is important to form some idea of the locality of the composition of the Gospel and Letters in order to be able to locate these writings within their proper social ecology and cultural-historical framework. Knowing the socio-historical context within which a document originated is essential for the effective under-standing of that particular document.

Obviously the question of locale is intimately linked to the whereabouts of the Johannine community. This complicates the issue, especially if one accepts that the Gospel was composed over a longer period of time. Such a view opens up the possibilities of considerably different scenarios. It might well be that during this long period of composition (that could have been 60 years) the community moved say from Palestine to Asia Minor, or that the authoritative figure behind the tradition could have been from a specific area, say Palestine, while the editors came from another area, say Ephesus. With all these variables the value of identifying the place of the final origin is relativized. In the case of the Letters it is a little easier. They do not have a long period of development and were written at a specific stage in the history of the community. The value of identifying their place of origin is of course considerably greater.

What are the possibilities for the locale in which the Gospel was composed, at least in its relatively final form?

(a) *Ephesus in Asia Minor.* The earliest traditions, like that of Irenaeus (*Adv. Haer.* 3.1.1) and Eusebius (*Ecol. Hist.* 3.23.1-4), link John and his Gospel to Ephesus. Internal evidence supports this external evidence. Some of the arguments are as follows. Tensions with the disciples of John the Baptist are evident, and the only place outside Palestine mentioned in the Bible where people were baptized with the baptism of John the Baptist is in Ephesus (Acts 19.1-7). The famous 'my Lord and God' pronouncement (20.28) would fit within the context of Caesar worship, which was important in Ephesus. There were Jewish communities in those areas that could explain the anti-Jewish trends in the Gospel. The anti-Gnostic polemic would also easily find a home in the Ephesus area, since Cerinthus, a Gnostic teacher, was at home in Ephesus at about 100 CE. There are no serious reasons why one could not locate it in Ephesus. None of these arguments are, however, so compelling that they could solve the problem of location conclusively.

In spite of some unanswered questions, like why John did not mention other Christian groups in the Ephesus area, the majority of scholars support Ephesus as the location of the Johannine community.

(b) *Alexandria in Egypt.* What counts in favour of Alexandria is that it was an academic centre that reckoned people like the Hermetic authors, Philo, and Valentinus, a famous Gnostic, among its citizens. Alexandria therefore is an ideal centre where diverse ideas could influence and form the thought world of the Johannine community. Such influence is evident in themes like the Johannine concept of *Logos*, the dualism, and also the expression of divinity. These arguments are stimulating but not convincing.

(c) *Syria or, perhaps more specifically, Antioch on the Orontes.* From very early on Antioch became the major centre for Christians outside Palestine (Acts 11). The main arguments in favour of Antioch as the locale where the Gospel took shape relate to thematic analogies between some Syrian writings and John's Gospel, or with the writings of a church father, Ignatius of Antioch, who resided here, or with the *Odes of Solomon* or even with some Gnostic writings. These arguments are very circumstantial and also failed to convince the scholarly world.

(d) *Northern Transjordan (areas of Batanea, Gaulanitis and Trachonitis).* Scholars favouring this area base their view on the nature of the conflict between the Jews and the Johannine community. Judaism in the first century was anything but homogeneous. The profile of the Jewish opponents in John's Gospel fits the type of synagogue Judaism found in Northern Transjordan under the rule of King Agrippa II. Wengst argues that the Johannine Christians fled there from Palestine with a vivid and independent memory of the teachings of Jesus, Jewish customs, and the geography of Palestine – which are all characteristics of the Gospel. Any developments in the theology could have taken place in this rather secluded atmosphere.

(e) *Different locations.* In light of the long period of composition of the Gospel, Brown as well as Schnackenburg keep the possibility open that the Johannine community could have migrated from Judaea/Galilee to the Transjordan area or could perhaps have travelled through Syria and from there to Ephesus. Once in Ephesus the tradition stabilized, was edited and resulted in the Gospel as we know it. This would explain the variety found in the Gospel, for instance, the sometimes accurate and sometimes inaccurate geographical and cultural information, the particular presentation of the Jews, or the independence from the synoptics.

Given these possibilities it seems as if the old tradition of Ephesus can still be accepted as a plausible location for the writing of the Gospel, bearing in mind that other places may have been at some or other stage part of the picture, due to the long period of composition.

What about the Letters? Well, their place of origin is of course directly linked to the location of the Johannine community at the end of the first century. If the Johannine community was located in Ephesus at the end of the first century, it seems logical that this would be the place of origin of the Letters. In any case, the Gnostic presence in Ephesus, of which Cerinthus was an example, would support this location.

3. Possible historical scenarios that prompted the composition of the Gospel and Letters

The purpose of John's Gospel and First Letter are usually stated in theological terms (20.31; 1 Jn 5.13): it was written so that people can believe (pastoral) or come to belief (missiological) in Jesus and by believing receive eternal life (soteriological). This implies that a reason for writing the Gospel was that there were people who had to be encouraged or convinced of the truth of the good news of Jesus Christ.

However, in chapter 4 above it was shown that the Gospel most probably developed over a longer period of time and that the Johannine group experienced several influences from the outside that could have prompted the way the Gospel was composed. What can be said about these influences? Many underlying reasons for writing the Gospel have been proposed by different scholars. I will mention just a few of these below.

(a)   The Gospel was written to correct views that exalted John the Baptist at the expense of Jesus. This would explain the subdued way in which the Gospel pictures John the Baptist (1.19-34; 3.25-30). At most, John the Baptist is presented as only a witness to Jesus.

(b)   Some argued that there was uneasiness with the way Jesus and his message were portrayed in the synoptics. The Gospel was therefore written to replace or supplement the synoptic Gospels. This would explain the different nature of John's Gospel compared to the others.

(c) The Gospel was written to support Samaritan claims of membership in the Christian faith (see chapter 4). The positive characterization of the Samaritans in the Gospel serves as the main argument for this view.

(d) The Gospel was written to correct certain theological emphases; for instance, the teaching on sacraments or eschatology. John does not mention the Eucharist, he also does not ask his disciples to baptize converts. This is seen as a reaction against these sacraments. Apart from that he emphasizes that whoever believes will have eternal life now (a realized eschatology), which is interpreted by some, on the basis of Jesus not returning as he said, as shifting the emphasis from expecting the future coming of Jesus to his presence here and now. These differences from the more orthodox views are seen by some as a reason for writing the Gospel.

(e) There are tendencies to see the Gospel as addressed to Christianity in general. No specific situation or group is really addressed. It is a sort of a-historical Gospel that addresses theological issues in general and can be read in any situation. The emphasis falls on the theological contents of the Gospel.

Although there is certainly some truth in each of these arguments, none of them can be regarded as the major reason for writing the Gospel.

An important clue for determining the historical framework within which these documents originated and grew is found in the references to conflict in the Gospel. The theology is developed within the context of, and determined by, a conflict between the 'disciples of Moses' and Johannine Christianity (called the 'disciples of Jesus'). (A brief note about the 'Jews' in the Gospel is necessary. The identity of the Jews is a widely discussed topic in recent literature. 'Jews' should not be identified with modern Jews, neither with all genealogical Jews in ancient times. Jesus and his disciples were also Jews. However, the term 'Jews' in the Gospel refers to a socio-religious category of people within the narrative of the Gospel who identify themselves as 'disciples of Moses' – 9.28.)

The Gospel reflects an intense dialogue between these two groups. It is not clear from the Gospel whether the dialogue was still going on or whether the split was already so deep that dialogue was not possible any longer. For instance, in John 9 the blind man is thrown out of the synagogue already and 15.18–16.2 points to serious conflict, while chapter 7 still indicates a possibility of some debate among the groups.

This is perhaps a reflection of the different stages in the development of the Gospel to its final form. How can this conflict be explained?

Among these Jewish people, who share a communal heritage (i.e. ancestry, Scriptures, prophets, the temple, etc.), a conflict developed that resulted in extreme opposition. The disciples of Jesus and the disciples of Moses both claimed to worship the same God, both are linked to the name 'Jews'; however, they respectively denied that the other group worshipped God. The major question underlying the conflict was, 'Where, and with whom, is God?' The conflict on the level of who God is in relation to Jesus and his opponents is clear from debates in, for example, 8.14-59 or 10.31-39. This is a question which was answered differently by the disciples of Jesus and the disciples of Moses, based on their differing convictions of who Christ was, each consequently claiming that God is on their side and that theirs is the only authentic religion. They indeed share a common heritage, but with the coming of Jesus the *locus* of God has changed. The history of God now continues in and with the followers of Jesus and not with the followers of Moses. Although the followers of Moses still had the physical Torah, still had a temple, still adhered to the purification rituals, still kept the Sabbath, and were very serious and diligent with their religion, their religion was empty and without God. God was now with Jesus – they were one (10.30). Cultic activities were no longer important, the importance now rested with the presence of God. If the followers of Moses therefore point to the law, or the temple, or purification jars, the followers of Jesus simply pointed out that it is not a physical building, but Jesus who now is the true temple (2.21); not water in purification jars purifies, but Jesus purifies (13.8; 15.2-3); both have the law but the law should be interpreted in the light of Jesus (5.39-40). The significant signs of the presence of God among his people in the past (like the law, temple, and so on) are all spiritually represented in Jesus now. And, what is the reason for this? All those signs of the presence of God simply pointed to God who was not visible. Now God is visible in Jesus – not the signs, but Jesus now stands in full focus if one asks where God is to be found. God is now the God that can be discovered, seen, and met in Jesus, to the extent that Jesus is not called a devil or blasphemer, but 'my Lord and my God' (20.28). The disciples of Jesus claim that if somebody does not accept the image and reality of God as it becomes present in Jesus, he or she is without God – this defines the essence of the conflict. This link between Jesus and the Jewish religious heritage aims to illustrate that Jesus is not introducing a new religion, but represents the continuation of the worship of the God of Israel.

Obviously these serious allegations from the followers of Jesus caused significant conflict among the two groups. The followers of Moses experienced it as blasphemy. This became clear when they crucified Jesus and chose to hate his followers with the same sentiment of rejection (15.18ff.).

To summarize: the theology of this Gospel is not formulated in an abstract, a-historical way. It is formulated to address the specific conflict the Johannine community experienced with the disciples of Moses. The basic question was where God was to be found. The Jewish opponents claimed that God was with them because of their relation to the Law, temple, and other cultic activities, their relation with Moses, or their ancestry through Abraham. The disciples of Jesus claimed that God was with them based on the revelation of Jesus. This is substantiated by his words and deeds and is attested to by Scripture. Accepting or rejecting this revelation is central to experiencing salvation or otherwise. Schematically it may be illustrated as in diagram 5.1.

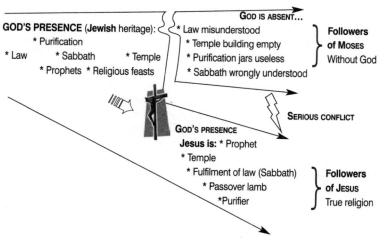

Diagram 5.1

If the historical scenario is accepted, the Gospel does not present a comprehensive, a-historical, all-inclusive theology, simply compiled for the sake of describing a comprehensive theology. Rather, it is a theology modelled on questions at stake in the conflict between the Johannine community and the 'Jews', namely, 'with whom is God and where can he be found (seen/heard)?' Furthermore, it addresses questions like how people in the midst of such a conflict can be encouraged to stay loyal to Jesus (a pastoral dimension) and how they can be strengthened in the conflict and continuing discourse with their opponents (missiological and apologetical dimensions).

In the Letters the conflict shifts to an inner-group conflict. The conflict with the opponents of Moses plays no role and little is seen of the dialogue with those outside of the Johannine group. The Johannine Christians are struggling among themselves in the Letters. 3 John suggests that the elder can still talk with some authority to the instigators of the conflict, 2 John 10 says one should close the door in the face of such a person, while 1 John points to a final break (1 Jn 2.18-19). This explains the emphasis on the Christological and ethical issues addressed in the Letters.

This prepares us for another important question. What were the socio-cultural and even historical influences on the author/editors of the Gospel that resulted in the particular ideas they expressed in these documents as well as their manner of formulating the message of Jesus the way they did?

6

Where Did the Author(s) of the Johannine Literature Get Their Ideas From?

1. The unique character of the Johannine literature

The composition history of the Gospel most probably covered a half a century with different editors and redactors working on the Gospel under different circumstances, as was explained in a previous chapter. It seems natural to accept that during this period those who brought the Gospel to its completion were exposed to different socio-religious and cultural influences. These influences are usually identified through the specific characteristics of the Gospel, for instance, its *dualism* that might suggest Persian, Jewish or even Gnostic involvement; the use of concepts like *Logos* (Word – 1.1) that might signify a conscious association with Hellenistic or Platonic socio-religious ecologies; the *mission* of Jesus that might perhaps be modelled on an existing (redeemer) myth from another religion.

For several reasons the origin and adaptation of ideas give rise to a highly complex issue. How do you answer questions like the following? Did the author rely on other ideas, and if so, which are they and where do they come from? Did the author(s) of the Gospel and Letters just copy other ideas or did these ideas indeed grow out of their community's deeper understanding of what the Gospel really means? Where does the idea come from that the king of the Jews will be God descending from above to die on earth before he ascends again, or that the Messiah will be the revelatory Word that is God? Moreover, how can you prove that such ideas came from a specific source if there are no quotations, or if you do not have that source any more? These are indeed difficult questions to answer.

If the author(s) of John's Gospel and Letters were influenced by ideas from different sources, a plausible theory must be offered on where they got these ideas from and why they accepted them as effective expressions of their Christian message. It was especially supporters of the *History of Religions* approach that made several suggestions about different religious influences that were formative on the Johannine literature as we have it today. Determining the influence of one document on another proved to be an elusive task, as the History of Religions practitioners soon realized. It resulted in identifying nearly every significant religious or philosophical movement in the ancient world as influential on John's ideas, only to later cast doubt on their own results, following further investigation. Different solutions were accepted in different periods of the previous century, although some sort of agreement grew in the latter part of the previous century and the beginning of this century that the socio-religious setting seems to be Jewish more than anything else.

2. Socio-religious influences: brief methodological considerations

The presupposition in comparing different religions is that different thought patterns of different religions influence one another. A chain-like developmental procedure is presupposed where an idea from a particular religion is taken up, reworked, adapted, and integrated into another religion. But how does one determine whether John's theology was influenced in this way? The major instrument is, of course, 'parallels' of some or other nature between the Gospel material and the material of the other religion. The most important ways of determining such influence on the Gospel through parallels are the following:

(a) *Literary* dependence means identifying the same sentences, phrases, words, etc. from the primary source in the secondary source. However, similar words do not necessarily point to direct dependence. They might contextually differ in meaning and could therefore not be seen as parallels, since within particular contexts ideas are interrelated with other words and therefore make sense in terms of these other words in that particular context. This results in difference in use and meaning. Contexts more than words should be paralleled. If the same word is used in both documents, it must be determined whether the contexts of the two writings at this point overlap and the intent of the language is comparable.

(b) *Thematical* links or parallels may also point to dependence. Again ideas must not only thematically overlap, but must function within the same contextual framework in both sources. It makes little sense to say that both documents make use of dualism, but that the dualisms are structurally different and function in different ways. There must be a strong contextual overlap between them.

Another methodological question is what the significance is of tracing influences of one religious source on the other.

Normally we interpret texts within the socio-cultural framework we deem appropriate for that text. Such a framework serves as a heuristic tool for interpreting the text. The further a text is separated from us, the more crucial it becomes to be aware of its socio-cultural ecology, since the gap between its intellectual framework and ours becomes wider and wider. This applies especially to the biblical documents. Their proper intellectual frameworks must be determined in order for us to understand them adequately. Identifying and using the wrong socio-cultural framework is the best recipe for misunderstanding.

The significance and influence of the religious ecology of, for instance, the Gospel of John become evident in a comparison between the commentaries of Bultmann and Brown. By suggesting that John's Gospel consists *inter alia* of a Gnostic source and reflects Gnostic ideas, Bultmann interprets the whole Gospel, even metaphors like water or images like the Good Shepherd or the True Vine, as Gnostic. Gnosticism becomes the lens through which the Gospel is read and that tints expressions and words. The same applies when assuming a Jewish socio-cultural ecology for the Gospel, like that employed by Brown – now the Good Shepherd or the true Vine are compared to, and read in the light of, Old Testament information. The *Logos* is not interpreted as a Gnostic redeemer, but is linked with Jewish wisdom, known from Proverbs already. The framework within which one reads a text is indeed crucial for the interpretation of that text. Arguments presented in this regard should be weighed thoroughly before a specific position is taken.

3. The possible socio-religious ecology of John's Gospel and Letters

The suggestions for the social ecology of John's Gospel and Letters cover a wide range of possibilities. In the previous century several prominent scholars, especially Bultmann, propagated Gnostic influences as a basic framework for understanding the Gospel. Others like Dodd favoured a Hellenistic background. However, in the latter part of the twentieth and beginning of the twenty-first century the focus shifted to Jewish literature that most probably influenced the Gospel and Letters. Let us briefly survey some of these suggestions.

3.1 Hellenism as the religious setting for John's Gospel and Letters

The Hellenistic culture was dominant at the time the Johannine literature was written, even in the Jewish capital Jerusalem itself. Judaism absorbed many Greek ideas during the Hellenistic period. This is evident from Jewish documents like the *Wisdom of Solomon* or *Jesus Sirach*. A Jerusalem Jew could have been influenced by Hellenism without even knowing it. This complicates the process of determining influences on John's Gospel and Letters. It is probable that the Johannine documents could have Hellenistic traits that are the result of Jewish influence instead of Greek influence.

Dodd (1953) and others argued that John's Gospel was strongly influenced by Hellenistic thought. Philo of Alexandria and a more philosophical religion from Egypt (fifth to second century BCE) known through literature as *Hermetica* were examples of such influences. Others even suggested more popular forms of Greek philosophy (Platonism or Stoicism).

Excursus: *Hellenism.* The Greek ruler Alexander the Great changed the political face of the ancient world at the end of the fourth century BCE (323 BCE). He conquered the powerful Persian Empire and was so impressed by the well-developed Persian culture that he followed a conscious policy of integration of Greek and Eastern Mediterranean cultural goods. What followed was the period known as Hellenism (ca. 200 BCE–100/200 CE). Hellenism was a combination of Greek philosophical, social and cultural ideas and those of the cultures of the ancient eastern Mediterranean world. The Greek rulers in Palestine, Egypt, Syria, Asia Minor and other areas were again serious about their own culture and indeed favoured integration of their culture in the areas they ruled. Nobody escaped this Hellenistic influence.

To get some feeling for this position, a few points of supposed contact between Hellenism and the Johannine literature are now given:

Dualism: Platonism, of course, starts with the distinction between realities: the earthly reality is only a shadow of the true spiritual reality above. Distinctions between realities found in John's Gospel (above/below – 3.31; flesh/spirit – 6.63) are therefore favourite proofs for such influence.

The wide usage of the word *Logos* (Word – 1.1) in ancient literature leads to virtually all the positions claiming it as proof for their influence on the Gospel. The use of *Logos* in the Gospel is seen by some as the result of Philo of Alexandria's influence, although this word was indeed a common term in Greek philosophy. However, closer scrutiny shows significant differences between John's use of the word, and the way it is employed in other contemporary religions, which questions direct dependence. Although similarities in vocabulary may be pointed out, direct influence from Hellenistic sources does not seem to be that convincing.

(a) In most cases the ideas in the Gospel that supposedly come directly from Hellenistic sources are not unique to Hellenism but were already shared by Judaism (like both the dualism and the idea of *Logos*). It might be that Judaism was originally influenced by these Hellenistic ideas, which means that it is more probable that John was indirectly exposed to the supposed Hellenistic ideas through its exposure to Jewish sources.

(b) In some cases the similarities are simply on the level of vocabulary (the same word is used) but not on the semantic level (the meaning of the word). The same word is used but with a completely different meaning. This is true of many comparisons with Philo and *Hermetica*.

(c) Some similarities may simply be explained as sharing the same religious ecology. For instance, Philo and John's Gospel shared their religious ecology with Judaism. No wonder there are similarities among them. In their formative stages they all drank from the same fountain but not necessarily from one another's sources.

Lately there have been some efforts to link some Johannine material (like sections of the Farewell Discourses) to Graeco-Roman practices and ideas, which might point to possible efforts in future to explore this framework again for overlaps or influence.

3.2 Docetistic and Gnostic influences

Gnosticism became prominent from the second century CE onwards. Nevertheless powerful proponents like Bultmann and his students maintained that the major influence on John's Gospel and Letters came from Gnosticism.

Excursus: *What is Gnosticism?* In the second century there were known Gnostic groups (e.g. Valentinians, Naassenes), but no single, clear description of them existed among the church fathers. Irenaeus' *Adversus Haereses* (1.21.1) seems to know a variety of such 'mystical doctrines'. A broad description would include the following. A radical cosmic dualism forms the framework of these ideas. On the basis of a myth of a being (*Demiurge*) who fell from the world of light, and created the world as well as the human beings, a view of reality resulted, distinguishing between the spiritual world as good, as opposed to the earthly, material world that was evil, bad, and hostile to God. Within this material world some (not all) humans have divine sparks (Gr. = *pneuma*) being kept captive within their material bodies. These divine sparks could only be freed through the revelation and enlightenment of divine knowledge (Gr. = *gnosis*), which must be mediated by a divine revealer. This knowledge will 'wake these divine sparks up' and lead them back to their spiritual origins. This might seem broadly compatible with Christian ideas, but the radical cosmic dualism implies a total devaluation of the earthly reality as being bad or evil. This has dramatic implications for one's view of humans. Jesus, for instance, could not have been human under such circumstances, since that would have meant that he was by definition evil. Salvation from sin is not necessary since self-discovery in the light of gained knowledge is salvific.

The exact definition of Gnosticism is however still debated. In the case of the church fathers the definition was narrow and until modern times Gnosticism was seen as restricted to early second-century Christian heresies. Lately this definition has broadened to include most ideas related to any form of secret knowledge, functioning within a dualistic framework. Such ideas were of course common in Hellenistic thought in general, and Gnosticism was then discovered by some as an ever-present phenomenon in the ancient religious ecology, based on this broader definition.

Something must be said about the sources we have of Gnostic material. Apart from the material in the church fathers (that is quite negative), little was known about Gnosticism. The discovery of the Nag Hammadi Library in Egypt changed this – these documents were buried round about the turn of the fourth and fifth centuries and were then discovered again in 1945. Thirteen codices (with 52 tractates – six duplicates) written in Coptic were discovered in this library and broadened the existing knowledge of Gnosticism considerably. The history of some of the documents seems to go back to the middle of the second century.

The influence of Gnosticism within Christianity was known since the apologetic writing of church fathers like Irenaeus (ca. 180 CE) who engaged in polemics against Gnosticism, based *inter alia* on the Gospel of John. However, in the previous century the debate was stimulated by prominent scholars like Bultmann and others (mostly his students). They favoured direct influence on the Gospel and Letters by Gnostic sources. This included the myth of a divine redeemer that descended from heaven. Other scholars did not support such a direct and radical influence of Gnosticism on John as Bultmann proposed. They acknowledged the presence of Gnostic ideas that influenced the New Testament in a limited way, but left the possibility open that the influence could have been indirect through Jewish sources (Schnackenburg). Others did not even go that far and just acknowledged similarity in vocabulary without trying to argue for any clear or significant influence. They even argued that John was not dependent on Gnostic material, but pre-empted it. Living in a Jewish world, influenced by Gnostic elements,

John's Gospel responded to these concerns. In all likelihood John had to struggle with similar questions and problems as those faced by the Gnostics and consequently used similar language, although in a different way (Lieu).

A major problem in the debate is that the first available Gnostic documents only date from the second century CE. From a literary point of view, it is problematic to claim that they influenced first-century New Testament documents that actually pre-date them. It should rather be the other way round, and many accept that Christianity influenced the emergence of Gnosticism, rather than the other way round.

Bultmann's source approach however helped him to argue for the priority of Gnosticism in the process of development, even though the Gnostic literary sources post-date the New Testament documents. He suggested that there were pre-literary elements of Gnosticism before the Christian documents came into being and could therefore influence Christian thought, although he could not produce such sources. Gnostic ideas were seen as free-floating (non-literary) sources available for religious movements even before Christianity, although they only found a solid basis for the development of their ideas in Christianity. Following Reitzenstein – who claimed that before Christianity there was a comprehensive worldview in existence that grew out of the combination of Oriental and Greek ideas – Bultmann argued that Gnosticism influenced Judaism in the form of Qumran before Christianity even existed. Bultmann's argument seems to be a bit circular, since he claims that the Gospel was influenced by Gnosticism, but then reconstructs Gnosticism from that very same Gospel. It was even argued by some that Christianity is Gnostic in its essence due to its initial reliance on Gnostic material. This is, however, highly unlikely since the differences are too great, especially when it comes to the dualism of the spiritual good and material evil.

The Johannine Gospel and Letters are seen by some as prime examples of formative Gnostic influences by the pro-Gnostic group. These ideas are still visible in the Gospel and Letters, although the author(s) thoroughly reworked them. Here are some examples of pro-Gnostic arguments:

(a) The use of concepts like *Logos* and *Paraclete* point to Gnostic influences. The *Paraclete* is seen as a Gnostic revealer. Obviously, this need not be the case, since both concepts can easily be explained within other socio-religious ecologies.

(b) The *Christology* of this Johannine corpus is also seen as being influenced by Gnostic elements. It is argued that the Son of man title is Gnosticized, based on his pre-existence and agency. Bultmann, for instance, maintains that there was a pre-Christian Gnostic myth of a divine figure that was sent down from the light to the demonically dominated darkness. He becomes human and reveals himself to people who were then divided into those who see and those who remain blind. Those who see start to long for their homeland in the world of light. Jesus instructs them on the way back to that desired destination and then returns there himself. This myth is then applied to Jesus and his story is told along those lines in John's Gospel. This argument was influential, but no longer enjoys wide acceptance, due to the circular nature of the argument and the lack of substantial literary proof.

Another Christological argument in favour of Gnostic influences was the 'high' Christology of the Gospel. Jesus is described in such divine and glorious terms that it is difficult to imagine that he could have been a human being. It is then suggested that his humanity was just a disguise through which his glorious divinity had to be revealed. Only his spiritual heavenly reality is important – this, of course, invites arguments in favour of Gnostic influence. This leads Käsemann to speak of a 'naive docetism' where Christ only appears to be a human.

(c) Johannine *dualism* (light–darkness; life–death) is presented in terms of cosmic enmity due to Gnostic influence. Even sections like John 10.1-18 and even 15.1-10, which probably have Old Testament roots, are also related to Gnostic myths. This implies that Gnostic influences were present, but had to be reworked significantly at several points.

On the other hand, there are also those who argue not for Johannine dependence on Gnostic material but the other way round: that Gnosticism was influenced by the Johannine literature. According to the early church fathers, such as Irenaeus, Gnosticism was a perversion of Christianity. It could be that Gnostic ideas were stimulated by, and received acceptance through, Christianity. Brown suggests a historical scenario in which the final edition of the Gospel appeared at the end of the first century. Some members of the community interpreted it in an 'incipiently Gnostic manner'. They believed that the world is saved by revelation instead of Jesus' death. Belief in the incarnation is what counts and not proper behaviour. 1 and 2 John were then written to refute these ideas, resulting in a split in the community. The opponents took their ideas as well as the Gospel with them into the movement that eventually grew into full Gnosticism. This would explain the popularity of John's Gospel in Gnostic circles. It seems that it was not by chance that the first commentary on John was written by a Valentinian Gnostic, or that the apologetic Irenaeus at the end of the second century tried to 'wrestle the Gospel back' into orthodox Christianity by using it in his anti-Gnostic apology.

There are also those who are of the opinion that John's Gospel had nothing to do with Gnosticism whatsoever. These two streams of thought could have developed separately and were indeed independent religious phenomena. At some stage, presumably at the end of the first century, the streams met, resulting in a partial synthesis among certain second-century groups. Only, from the second century onwards, the Johannine literature was reinterpreted and used by Gnostics in their debates.

The Gnostic debate is still clouded by many unsolved questions. The definitions are not that clear, the origin of the ideas or sources are equally vague, the relationship between John's material and Gnostic material is to a large extent hypothetical, because of the lack of proper comparative material, for example. What we do know, thanks especially to the discovery of the Gnostic documents in the Nag Hammadi Library, in the previous century, is that there was a movement of Gnostics from the second century onwards and they had a special affinity for John's material.

Be that as it may, after the strong Bultmannian pro-Gnostic wave, the water has calmed down in the wake of another wave – the pro-Judaistic wave, stimulated by influential books like the impressive commentary of Raymond Brown. The idea of a fully developed myth of a Gnostic redeemer that influenced John's view of Jesus has subsided with this Gnostic wave. Jewish material, especially parallels from the Old Testament, are now favoured for explaining the Johannine conceptual and linguistic world. More complicated and longer explanations involving Gnostic material are no longer deemed necessary, or even the best way of explaining the Johannine material.

3.3 Judaism in various forms

The narrative setting of the Gospel is thoroughly Jewish – the events took place in Galilee, as well as in Jerusalem and surroundings. The Greeks only appear on the scene at the end of Jesus' public ministry (12.20). Up to that point Jesus' interaction is just with Jews (except for the Samaritans in chapter 4). The narrative framework is Jewish – there are, for instance, the temple in Jerusalem, Jewish feasts, arguments about the finer detail of interpreting the Law of Moses, or the expectations among the Jews of prophets who will return, well-known Old Testament imagery like the shepherd or vine, as well as ample references to the fulfilment of the Old Testament. Given this framework, it is no surprise that the Jewish socio-religious ecology is favoured by the majority of scholars today, obviously still acknowledging some other influences here and there in the Gospel material. Attention shifted to the Jewish religious ecology in the period after Bultmann.

Having said this, one must immediately recognize that first-century Judaism was not a single, unified group. The Jews were taken into Babylonian captivity in the East. Many remained there when Ezra and Nehemiah later returned to rebuild Jerusalem in the fifth century BCE. Once back in Israel they were under religious, cultural and political pressure from the Hellenists and later the Romans. Assimilation on economic or political levels placed immense pressure on integration on the religious level too, or at least of adapting one's own ideas or even introducing some new ideas. Not all Jews reacted in the same way to these challenges. Some were in favour of integration with foreign cultures (mainly for political and economic reasons), while others followed a more 'conservative' line and tried to stay as close as possible to traditional Jewish practices at the time of Jesus. Judaism(s) indeed stretched from virtually accepting Hellenism *en toto* to a more balanced interaction with Hellenism, to a rejection of Hellenism and a withdrawal into a (orthodox/traditional) Judaism that tried to stay 'pure' from Hellenistic influences (as far as that was possible – even here there were different groups, each one trying to outclass the other in their 'pureness'), basing their positions more on the Old Testament than anything else.

A further complicating factor was that the Jews were spread across the known ancient world – at the time of Jesus it is estimated that there were more Jews outside of Palestine than in Palestine. They did not always have contact with the 'headquarters' as long as it was situated in or around Jerusalem (Jerusalem was destroyed in 70 CE). This inevitably contributed to the syncretistic variety within first-century Judaism. The Jews had so long been in contact with Hellenism that Judaism was indelibly marked by Hellenistic influences, even in Palestine. This poses the question: bearing this varied Judaism in mind, where did the influences on the Johannine literature come from?

Interestingly enough, the picture of the 'Jews' in the Gospel itself is rather unified. Although there are several descriptions of the different groups, for instance, the Pharisees (1.24), priests (1.19), Levites (1.19), chief priests (7.32, 45), people of Jerusalem (7.25) or simply crowds (7.12), and there are some geographical divisions and stereotyping (1.46; 4.43-45; 7.41-42, 52 – Jerusalem vs. Galilee/Nazareth), the 'Jews' are presented as a 'unified group' under strict authority of their leaders in Jerusalem. They are even identified according to clear characteristics: they are diligent readers of scripture because they are believed to have eternal life in them (5.39), they are followers of Moses and the Law (1.17; 9.28), their religious and social life centres not only around the temple but also in and around the synagogue (9.22; 16.2). They seem to have been a group attached to the synagogue who were serious about the Law of Moses and who were passionate about keeping their religion in line with their Mosaic tradition. Obviously not all the different groups in Judaism are intended to be identified with the 'Jews' in the Gospel of John, as is evident from the precise description of the qualities of the Jewish opponents in the Gospel. The challenge is therefore to match the qualities of the 'Jews' in the Gospel with a particular group within the wider and diverse Judaism as it manifested itself during the time of the origin of the Gospel.

Some scholars, like Cullmann, argued that the Johannine community should be placed within syncretistic marginal Judaism, similar to the people who are identified as 'Hellenists' in Acts 6. Other influences from Qumran Judaism and the Samaritans merged with the Hellenistic influences and resulted in what we have in the Gospel.

However, it is the more traditional forms of Judaism that provide the best parallels to what we have in this Gospel. The frequent use of and reference to the Old Testament, the strong links to the synagogue and the emphasis on the Sabbath and Law, points to the more traditional type of Judaism where Hellenism was not consciously adopted or supported. This seems to be the Jewish socio-religious ecology of John's Gospel. What evidence do we have for this statement?

The Jewish socio-religious ecology is best known from their scriptures. The *Old Testament* as expression of the Jewish religious traditions plays an important role in the Gospel. Although quotations from scripture (Old Testament) in this Gospel are varied in nature and apparently mainly come from Greek translations, it cannot be denied that the thought world of the Old Testament forms an important framework for the thought patterns of John's Gospel. The scriptures were held in high regard and are called the Word of God in 10.34. Let us briefly investigate.

Thematically the Gospel seems to be drenched in Old Testament themes, like the prominence of Moses, the Law and the manna (3.14; 5.45-47; 6.31ff.), the implicit and explicit references to Abraham (8.39, 58) or Jacob (1.51; 4.5-6), quotations from Isaiah (12.37-41) and the fulfilment of Old Testament prophecies, the Passover and other Jewish festive motifs; and Jesus as the creative Word (*Logos* – 1.1-3) is associated with Jewish Wisdom. Although the descent-ascent of God's agent (Jesus' mission) was one of the major pro-Gnostic arguments, the mission of prophets in the Old Testament serves as a better framework for understanding the mission of Jesus, the Prophet. Sections like John

10 (Good Shepherd) and 15 (True Vine), that Bultmann interpreted from a Gnostic perspective, are better understood in the light of similar Old Testament imagery. Even the use of the 'I am'-sayings may be interpreted in the light of Deutero-Isaiah.

These close affinities to the Old Testament, which according to Hengel appear on all levels of the thought in this Gospel, suggest a community that took the scriptures seriously and applied them to their everyday situation – indeed more traditional Jewish than Hellenistic emphases are evident in this regard.

There was, however, some hesitancy about the Jewish origin of the *Johannine dualism* (light/darkness; life/death), since it was thought that such a dualism was not Jewish but rather Persian/Hellenistic/Gnostic. The discovery of the Dead Sea Scrolls at Qumran in 1947 changed the whole scene and served as a major impetus to place John's Gospel within a Jewish ecology. The so-called Qumran community settled at the shores of the Dead Sea more or less in the middle of the second century BCE until the settlement was destroyed in 68 CE. This community gives us some insight into one of the forms of Judaism during this period. The Qumran documents were proof that Persian and Hellenistic ideas were indeed integrated into even more conservative forms of Judaism.

In Jewish documents from Qumran a dualistic worldview is also evident, which means that it is no longer necessary to look for influences outside of Jewish Palestine when trying to explain the presence of dualism in the Gospel of John. As it happens, not only the idea of dualism, but also vocabulary was shared by some Qumran documents and John's Gospel. For instance, in Qumran literature concepts are found like the prince of *lights* that overpowers the angel of *darkness*, as well as the contrast between truth and falsehood. The teacher of righteousness of the Qumran community is paralleled with Jesus, and the *Paraclete* as a forensic figure is linked with intercessory agents in Qumran, especially Michael, the spirit of truth. The importance of loyalty and love towards one's community are shared by both John's community and that of Qumran. Although scholars are hesitant to propose direct influence, since there is not one direct known literary parallel between John's Gospel and the Qumran documents, indirect influences are often suggested.

It is, however, the differences between the Qumran documents and John's Gospel that call for some caution. Often the vocabulary does not overlap and when it does, the words often do not carry the same meaning. The purpose and focus of the documents are also not the same. Qumran and Johannine Christianity were two different communities that perhaps shared a religious ecology, which means that direct influence or dependence should not be postulated. Perhaps the link between the two communities could have been the ex-disciples of John the Baptist who turned Christian, and who might have had associations with the Qumran (Essene?) movement.

Then there is *rabbinical* literature. The ideas of the Pharisees/rabbis that became prominent after the destruction of the temple were only written down from the second century onwards. This makes it difficult to relate the rabbinical literature directly to John's Gospel. Nevertheless, it cannot be denied that the roots of the rabbinical ideas lie in the first century already and that these people had a strong and practical mentality for preserving tradition. After the destruction of the temple in 70 CE the Pharisaic ideas grew in prominence and were seen as a unifying force in Judaism. Strack and Billerbeck especially present us with many parallels, which must be treated with care, but should not be ignored. Borgen's influential book on John 6 as rabbinic *midrashim* has underlined the links between John and rabbinic Judaism. He even links the Agent motif in John's Gospel to rabbinic agency models. Obviously, the term *Logos* is also seen as a connecting term between Wisdom literature and rabbinic literature. Be this as it may, such links again point to a religious ecology on the traditional Jewish side rather than on the Hellenistic side.

4. Conclusion

What should we make of all these suggestions? The picture remains complex, but the following may serve as a broad indication of what should be regarded as possible.

Although the debate will surely continue, it seems that the religious ecology of John's ideas is varied – no single influence can be isolated, but it is rather a matter of convergence of different influences. The major area of similarity lies within traditional Judaism that takes the Old Testament and the Law seriously. Within this framework special interest was shown in Wisdom literature that was influenced not only by Proverbs but also by the more Hellenistic *Ben Sirach* or *Wisdom of Solomon*. Some sort of relation – most probably indirect – with the thought patterns of Qumran could be reckoned with. There are also individual elements that might be explained in the light of Hellenistic philosophy or even Gnostic ideas, although the relationship between these ideas is not necessarily direct. It could be explained from a shared religious ecology. This option should only be used if it could not be explained within a Jewish perspective.

However, an important fact to remember is that John did not copy or rewrite any other document, not even the synoptics. He was a creative author, and the presentation of his ideas was influenced mainly by the Jesus tradition within which he stood and which he represented. Within this tradition he integrated, transformed and reworked other influences to express his message in his own unique way. This underlines the importance of first getting to know the contents of the text before concluding that a particular background is the framework for interpreting that particular text. Choosing a particular socio-cultural ecology should explain as many as possible of the phenomena in the text. One will only know whether a particular socio-cultural ecology explains the text adequately if one knows the text in its inter-relatedness well. This was the rationale behind the structure of this book.

Conclusion: Johannine Literature Today

This book started with the remark that reading Johannine documents is an exciting adventure that takes one on diverse roads, and we have indeed experienced that – the Johannine documents can at once seem straightforward to understand but simultaneously surprise you with their depth and finesse of expression and ideas. We came to understand the old expression that dates back to the time of the church fathers, namely, that a baby can play in the pool of the Johannine literature, while at the same time an elephant could drown in it. That is why the Johannine literature will never lose its attraction for its readers. Some will read it for its theological depth, others for its refined literary strategies, others out of curiosity ... but it will be read.

From a scholarly point of view we have seen that the pendulum is constantly on the move when it comes to the interpretation of these documents. It moves between Gnostic, Hellenistic and Jewish frameworks; from documents containing several sources to documents that must be read as single units; from general messages to all Christians to documents that are aimed at specific groups; and so one can go on. The advantage of this movement of the pendulum is of course that the study of the Johannine literature becomes more refined with each successive movement. More possibilities are considered and the strengths and weaknesses of each position are more carefully scrutinized. The danger, however, is that the same known material or knowledge is repeated in each article after the next. Sadly, this happens far too frequently in Johannine scholarship. To move forward the Johannine scholar should take cognizance of the state of knowledge regarding this corpus of literature. This book tried to draw broad lines of some of the essential knowledge that is available in order to illustrate how they are interrelated. Be that as it may, there is a constant challenge to explore Johannine material further and in this quest for clearer understanding there is indeed place enough for many further worthy and novel contributions.

Academic reading in the middle of the previous century was dominated by discussions about sources and their origins (Gnostic, Hellenistic, Qumran). As was indicated, this obviously influenced the way the message of the Gospel was interpreted. Lately, the focus has moved to the literary characteristics of the Gospel. The result is that the text as a unit increasingly stands in the centre of contemporary research. Theological issues relating to the text have naturally received more focus as a result of this shift, since focusing on the text, or its narrative structure, leads to the message of the Gospel. However, no single approach or issue could be considered to dominate Johannine research at the beginning of the twenty-first century. Obviously, in some circles there is a stronger focus on the literary issues, while historical questions keep on inspiring other researchers. A constant flow of research ranging from radical reception theories to rather fundamentalistic theological approaches is a common characteristic of contemporary Johannine research. Because of the multifaceted nature of the Gospel this tendency will continue. As a result, Johannine research may be compared with a Chinese rice field. The text of the Gospel is worked, and has been reworked for centuries now. The challenge of the present-day researcher is either to expand the field a little or to find a spot in the field that was missed by previous workers.

Academics will continue to read the Gospel, but so will other readers that have little interest in academic concerns. Believers will continue to draw inspiration from the encouraging message that the Father and Son are with them, and within them, guiding them through the Spirit-*Paraclete*. The unique way in which John explains the wondrous nature of the Son will continue to be a firm foundation to the confessions of churches, as it was for centuries. And while the Johannine Gospel and Letters are read by interested people, the digging in the Chinese rice field will continue, giving each of the workers a great deal of satisfaction after the hard day's work.

Further Reading and Bibliography

This list contains books that were referred to in the text itself, as well as books that can be suggested for further reading. To compile a representative list of Johannine literature is close to impossible. Books mentioned here may serve as a point of departure for those who want to pursue particular issues.

Useful commentaries

Barrett, C.K. 1978 *The Gospel according to St John*. Philadelphia: Westminster.
Beasley-Murray, G.R. 1987 *John*. WBC 36; Waco: Word.
Brown, R.E. 1966–71 *The Gospel according to John: Introduction, Translation and Notes*. 2 vols. Garden City: Doubleday.
Brown, R.E. 1983 *The Epistles of John*. Garden City: Doubleday.
Bultmann, R. 1971 *The Gospel of John*. Philadelphia: Westminster.
Carson, D.A. 1991 *The Gospel according to John*. Grand Rapids: Eerdmans.
Klauck, H.-J. 1991 *Der erste Johannesbrief*. Zurich: Benziger Verlag.
Lindars, B. 1972 *The Gospel of John*. London: Oliphants.
Marshall, I.H. 1978 *The Epistles of John*. Grand Rapids: Eerdmans.
Moloney, F.J. 1998 *The Gospel of John*. Collegeville: Liturgical Press.
Schnackenburg, R. 1968–84 *The Gospel according to St John* (4 vols). London: Burns & Oates.
Schnackenburg, R. 1992 *The Johannine Epistles*. Tunbridge Wells: Burns & Oates.
Thyen, H. 2005 *Das Johannesevangelium*. Tübingen: Mohr Siebeck.
Wengst, K. 2000 *Das Johannesevangelium*. Stuttgart: Kohlhammer.

Other Literature

Ashton, J. 1993 *Understanding the Fourth Gospel*. Oxford: Clarendon Press.

Bailey, J.A. 1963 *The Traditions Common to the Gospels of Luke and John*. Leiden: Brill.

Bauckham, R. (ed.) 1998 *The Gospels for All Christians: Re-thinking the Gospel Audiences*. Grand Rapids: Eerdmans.

Becker, J. 2004 *Johanneisches Christentum. Seine Geschichte und theologie im Überblick*. Tübingen: Mohr Siebeck.

Bieringer, R. et al. (eds) 2001 *Anti-Judaism and the Fourth Gospel*. Louisville: Westminster John Knox.

Boismard, M.-É. 1962 'Saint Luc et la redaction du quatrième évangile'. *RB* 69, 185–211.

Borgen, P. 1981 *Bread from Heaven. An Exegetical Study of the Concept of Manna in the Gospel of John and the Writings of Philo*. Leiden: Brill.

Brown, R.E. 1979 *The Community of the Beloved Disciple*. New York: Paulist Press.

Brown, R.E. 2003 *An Introduction to the Gospel of John*. New York: Doubleday.

Bultmann, R. 1955 *Theology of the New Testament*. London: SCM Press.

Cullmann, O. 1976 *The Johannine Circle: Its Place in Judaism, Among the Disciples of Jesus and in Early Christianity*. London: SCM Press.

Culpepper, R.A. 1983 *Anatomy of the Fourth Gospel: A Study in Literary Design*. Philadelphia: Fortress.

Culpepper, R.A. 1998 *The Gospel and Letters of John*. Nashville: Abingdon Press.

De Boer, M. 1996 *Johannine Perspectives on the Death of Jesus*. Kampen: Pharos.

Dodd, C.H. 1953 *Interpretation of the Fourth Gospel*. Cambridge: Cambridge University Press.

Dodd, C.H. 1963 *Historical Tradition in the Fourth Gospel*. Cambridge: Cambridge University Press.

Du Rand, J.A. 1991 *Johannine Perspectives*. Pretoria: Orion.

Edwards, R.B. 1996 *The Johannine Epistles*. Sheffield: Sheffield Academic Press.

Forestell, T. 1974 *The Word of the Cross*. Rome: Biblical Institute.

Fortna, R.T. 1970 *The Gospel of Signs: A Reconstruction of the Narrative Source Underlying the Fourth Gospel*. Cambridge: Cambridge University Press.

Fortna, R.T. 1988 *The Fourth Gospel and Its Predecessor: From Narrative Source to Present Gospel*. Philadelphia: Fortress

Frey, J. 1997–2000 *Die johanneische Eschatologie*. Vols 1–3, Tübingen: Mohr Siebeck.

Gardner-Smith, P. 1938 *Saint John and the Synoptics*. Cambridge: Cambridge University Press.

Goppelt, L. 1982 *Theology of the New Testament*. Grand Rapids: Eerdmans.

Guthrie, D. 1981 *New Testament Theology*. Leicester: InterVarsity Press.

Hägerland, T. 2003 'John's Gospel: A Two-Level Drama?' *JSNT 25*, 309–22.

Hahn, F. 2002 *Theologie des Neuen Testaments*. Vols 1–2. Tübingen: Mohr Siebeck.

Hengel, M. 1989 *The Johannine Question*. London: SCM Press.

Käsemann, E. 1968 *The Testament of Jesus according to John 17*. London: SCM Press.

Koester, C. 1995 *Symbolism in the Fourth Gospel*. Minneapolis: Fortress.

Kümmel, W.G. 1976 *Theology of the New Testament*. London: SCM Press.

Kysar, R. 1975 *The Fourth Evangelist and His Gospel: An Examination of Contemporary Scholarship*. Minneapolis: Augsburg Press.

Kysar, R. 1985 'The Fourth Gospel: A Report on Recent Research' in *Aufstieg und Niedergang der Römischen Welt*, ed. W. Haase. Vol. 25.3. Berlin: De Gruyter, 2391–2465.

Kysar, R. 1993 *The Maverick Gospel*. Louisville: Westminster John Knox.

Lindars, B. 1971 *Behind the Fourth Gospel*. London: SPCK.

Lieu, J.M. 1991 *The Theology of the Johannine Epistles*. Cambridge: Cambridge University Press.

Martyn, J.L. 1968 *History and Theology in the Fourth Gospel*. Louisville: Westminster John Knox.

Menken, M.J.J. 1996 *Old Testament Quotations in the Fourth Gospel: Studies in Textual Form*. Kampen: Kok.

Moody Smith, D. 1995 *The Theology of the Gospel of John*. Cambridge: Cambridge University Press.

Morris, L. 1995 *The Gospel According to John*. NICNT; Grand Rapids: Eerdmans.

Neirynck, F. et al. (eds) 1979 *Jean et les Synoptiques: Examen critique de l'exégèse de M.-É. Boismard*. Leuven: Leuven University Press.

Painter, J. 1991 *The Quest for the Messiah: The History, Literature and*

Theology of the Johannine Community. Edinburgh: T&T Clark.

Perkins, P. 1990 'John's Gospel and Gnostic Christologies: The Nag Hammadi Evidence', *ATR* Supplement 11, 68–76.

Robinson, J.A.T. 1985 *The Priority of John*. London: SCM Press.

Sabbe, M. 1991 *Studia Neotestamentica: Collected Essays*. Leuven: Leuven University Press.

Schnelle, U. 1987 *Antidoketische Christologie im Johannesevangelium: Eine Untersuchung zur Stellung des vierten Evangeliums in der johanneischen Schule*. Göttingen: Vandenhoeck & Ruprecht.

Schnelle, U. 1998 *Das Evangelium nach Johannes*. Leipzig: Evangelische Verlagsanstalt.

Smalley, S.S. 1998 *John – Evangelist and Interpreter*. Carlisle: Paternoster.

Stibbe, M.G.W. 1994 *John as Storyteller: Narrative Criticism and the Fourth Gospel*. Cambridge: Cambridge University Press.

Strack, H.L. and Billerbeck, P. 1978 *Kommentar zum Neuen Testament aus Talmud und Midrash*. Munich: Beck.

Talbert, C.H. 1992 *Reading John: A Literary and Theological Commentary on the Fourth Gospel and the Johannine Epistles*. London: SPCK.

Theobald, M. 1992 *Gott, Logos und Pneuma. 'Trinitarische' Rede von Gott im Johannesevangelium* in *Monotheismus und Christologie. Zur Gottesfrage im hellenistischen Judentum und im Urchristentum*, ed. H.-J. Klauck. Freiburg: Herder, 41–87.

Thompson, M.M. 2001 *The God of the Gospel of John*. Grand Rapids: Eerdmans.

Van Belle, G. 1988 *Johannine Bibliography 1966–1985*. Leuven: Peeters.

Van Belle, G. 1994 *The Signs Source in the Fourth Gospel: Historical Survey and Critical Evaluation of the Semeia Hypothesis*. Leuven: Lueven University Press.

Van der Horst, P.W. 2000 'Korte notities over het godsbegrip bij Grieken en Romeinen en de vergoddelijking van Jezus in het Niewuwe Testament' in *Mozes, Plato, Jezus. Studies over de wereld van het vroege Christendom*. Amsterdam: Prometheus, 79–86.

Van der Watt, J.G. 2000 *Family of the King: Dynamics of Metaphor in the Gospel according to John*. Leiden: Brill.

Van der Watt, J.G. 2005 'Salvation according to the Gospel of John' in *Salvation in the New Testament: Perspectives on Soteriology*, ed. J.G. Van der Watt. Leiden: Brill.

Zimmermann, R. 2004 *Christologie der Bilder im Johannesevangelium.* Tübingen: Mohr Siebeck.

Zumstein, J. 1999 *Kreative Erinnerung. Relecture und Auslegung im Johannesevangelium.* Zurich: Pano.